T0299785

Between Systems and Violence

Between Systems and Violence offers a compilation and analysis of state-level statutes targeting intimate partner violence (IPV) in immigrant and/or refugee (IMR) lives. The book analyzes such statutes' legal language via various theoretical lenses, as well as provides a discussion of implications for research, prevention, intervention, and public policy.

Some IMR victim-survivors of IPV, such as those who are undocumented, may be pinned "between systems and violence" as violent partners use the immigration system as a mechanism of power and control. While protections are available for these victim-survivors, the story told about the encompassing legal landscape remains incomplete and relegated to federal law.

Graduate students, as well as scholars and practitioners, will acquire an in-depth understanding of this important nexus.

Julio Montanez, BA, is a graduate student at the University of Central Florida (UCF) and serves as a Project Manager in the UCF Institute for Social and Behavioral Science. His research generally focuses on the intersection of intimate partner violence (IPV) and law/policy.

Amy Donley, PhD, is an Associate Professor in the Department of Sociology at the University of Central Florida (UCF) and the Director of the UCF Institute for Social and Behavioral Sciences. She is an applied sociologist whose research primarily focuses on social inequalities, specifically food insecurity, urban poverty, and homelessness. She regularly conducts research in partnership with local governments and not-for-profit agencies.

Amy Reckdenwald, PhD, is an Associate Professor in the Department of Sociology at the University of Central Florida (UCF) and a member of the UCF Violence Against Women Faculty Cluster. Her research primarily focuses on violent victimization and offending; particularly as it relates to domestic violence and intimate partner homicide.

Routledge Studies in Crime and Society

Between Systems and Violence

State-Level Policy Targeting
Intimate Partner Violence in
Immigrant and Refugee Lives

**Julio Montanez, Amy Donley,
and Amy Reckdenwald**

Routledge
Taylor & Francis Group

NEW YORK AND LONDON

First published 2022
by Routledge
605 Third Avenue, New York, NY 10158

and by Routledge
4 Park Square, Milton Park, Abingdon, Oxon, OX14 4RN

Routledge is an imprint of the Taylor & Francis Group, an informa business

Library of Congress Cataloging-in-Publication Data
A catalog record for this title has been requested

ISBN: 978-0-367-76376-3 (hbk)
ISBN: 978-0-367-76469-2 (pbk)
ISBN: 978-1-003-16704-4 (ebk)

DOI: 10.4324/9781003167044

To all victims and survivors.

Contents

x *Contents*

Acknowledgments

The authors first wish to acknowledge and thank Brian Hall, a graduate student in the Department of Sociology at the University of Central Florida. Brian conducted literature searches that helped the authors obtain an understanding of the extant literature on multiple topics within this book. Thank you so much, Brian.

The authors also wish to acknowledge and thank Amanda Koontz, PhD. Professor Koontz provided readings and preliminary ideas that formed the starting point for Chapter 5 of this book. Thank you so much, Professor Koontz.

Finally, the authors wish to acknowledge and thank the Funding, Professional Development, and Scholarship department of the UCF College of Graduate Studies. This department offers the UCF Summer Mentoring Fellowship, which provided the first author of this book with the time, structure, and space to make substantial progress on this book's contents.

1 Introduction

Intimate partner violence (IPV) includes "physical violence, sexual violence, stalking, and psychological aggression (including coercive tactics) by a current or former intimate partner" (Breiding, Basile, Smith, Black, & Mahendra, 2015, p. 11). In addition to including various types (e.g., physical, sexual) and relationship classifications (e.g., spousal, dating), IPV also includes other dimensions. According to Montanez, Donley, and Reckdenwald (2020), this means that each episode or pattern of IPV has:

- A severity through which violence hurts.
- A frequency through which violence recurs.
- A duration through which violence lasts.
- A number of perpetrators through which violence can reappear across the lifespan.

These factors combine to form multidimensional violent constellations (see Hamby & Grych, 2013; Scott-Storey, 2011; Thompson et al., 2006; see also Montanez et al., 2020).

The extant IPV figures are staggering. In 2018, 3 out of every 1000 people aged 12 and older in the United States (U.S.) experienced IPV in the past year (Morgan & Oudekerk, 2019). Across the lifespan, intimate partner physical violence, contact sexual violence, and/or stalking have befallen approximately 80 million[1] men and women (Smith et al., 2018). Included in these statistics are immigrant and refugee (IMR) populations. Indeed, for some IMR victim-survivors of IPV, the tug-of-war between staying in an abusive relationship and facing potential legal consequences, like deportation, reveals a difficult reality (see, e.g., Erez & Harper, 2018). In the U.S., the national-level policy has been implemented in an attempt to lessen these difficulties and help IMR victim-survivors of IPV attain freedom from abuse (see Erez &

DOI: 10.4324/9781003167044-1

Harper, 2018; Orloff & Kaguyutan, 2002). Left undiscussed within the extant literature is policy targeting IPV against IMR persons across the U.S.'s major subnational units. Accordingly, the present research analyzes state-level statutes targeting IPV against IMR persons.

The present research contributes to a better understanding of IPV in IMR lives through multiple avenues. First, the research provides an interdisciplinary and theoretically grounded analysis of the intersection of two phenomena: IPV and immigration systems (for a discussion of the intersection, see, e.g., Erez & Harper, 2018). Second, looking at state-level policy in general can reveal the interaction between societal attitudes and government outputs (see, e.g., Lax & Phillips, 2009). Third, individualist attitudes that separately target battered women and immigrants (e.g., "Go back to your country!" or "Why does she stay?"; Aratani, 2019; Kelly, 2011), like stereotypes, redirect attention away from the system level (Davies et al., 2015). Accordingly, such an analysis presents an opportunity to treat systems, not victims (Pence & Paymar, 1993). Thus, interrogating structures can help to expose the broader forces that construct status. In this way, the present research obtains an understanding of how policy shapes the statuses of IMR victim-survivors of IPV.

Intimate Partner Violence

Statistics

Gender and Violence Types

The story of physical IPV in national-level statistics is complicated. Indeed, early extant research galvanized a debate between (a) finding equal spousal physical IPV rates between men and women (see Straus & Gelles, 1989; Straus, Gelles, & Steinmetz, 1980) and (b) women's victimization at higher rates than men (see Tjaden & Thoennes, 2000). However, nuanced explanations for the role of gender in IPV arose over time, including the implications of coercive controlling violence and the varied detection of certain violence configurations across general survey and agency samples (see Johnson, 2008; Kelly & Johnson, 2008). More recent research shows physical IPV dynamics to be more complex. While in general physical violence seems to be gender symmetric, severity and overlap with other violence types paint a more nuanced picture. At the national level, the prevalence of actions such as slapping, pushing, and shoving tends to be roughly more similar between genders than in other forms (see Smith et al., 2018). For example, 2010 national-level data show that slapping was reported among a slightly greater percentage of women (20.4 percent) than men (18.3 percent). On the other hand, women experience higher rates of more severe physical IPV (Breiding et al., 2014; Smith et al., 2018). For example, 9.7 percent of women versus 1.1 percent of men reported experiencing choking (i.e., strangling) or suffocating by an intimate partner; 17.2 percent and 2.7 percent of women and men, respectively, reported being slammed against something; 10.4 percent and 2.9 percent of women and men, respectively, reported experiencing hair-pulling (see Breiding et al., 2014). Looking more intricately, research has shown that experiencing physical violence *alone* overwhelmingly features male victimization (92 percent) when compared to female victimization (56.8 percent), and more women than men experience the intersection of physical violence and stalking (14.4 percent and 6.3 percent, respectively; see Breiding et al., 2014). As an unwanted and fear-inducing pattern, stalking involves the harassment and threatening of a partner. According to the National Intimate Partner and Sexual Violence Survey (NISVS), intimate partner stalking affected 10.4 percent and 2.2 percent of women and men, respectively (Smith et al., 2018).

Sexual violence constitutes another IPV type. Tactics utilized in these situations can include coerced sexual activities based on force or threatening harm on a person the victim knows (see Tjaden & Thoennes, 2000). Experiences of intimate partner sexual violence have affected 18.3 percent of women and 8.2 percent of men, according to the NISVS (Smith et al., 2018). National Crime Victimization Survey (NCVS) data show that over the course of 10 years, rape/sexual assault against intimates has plagued 9.6 percent of women and 1.2 percent of men (Catalano, 2013). Moreover, sexual IPV is often accompanied by other violence types (Krebs, Breiding, Browne, & Warner, 2011), such as psychological violence.

Psychological aggression can be divided into two subtypes: expressive aggression and coercive control (Smith et al., 2018). A great deal of the IPV literature has historically focused on topics of power, control, and coercion. Grounded in the Power and Control Wheel, these constructs revolve around forceful imbalances of influence within a relationship, such that physical and sexual violence can form perpetuating points for tactics, like isolation, that systematically dismantle personal autonomy (Pence & Paymar, 1993). According to the 2015 NISVS, coercive control rates against women and men were roughly equal (30.6 percent and 29.8 percent, respectively). However, breaking down the statistics further shows that women experience more victimization that includes control over money, not being allowed to see family and friends, and threats of physical harm. Men experience more controlling victimization that includes being monitored by the violence-perpetrating partner (Smith et al., 2018).

*Intersecting Violent Dimensions, Violence
Tools, and Violent Death*

IPV is also an example of "intersecting dimensions of violence, abuse, and victimization" (see Figure 1.1; Montanez et al., 2020). That is, IPV's contributing parts, like severity and frequency, form cross-sections that multiply to form violent constellations (see Montanez et al., 2020; Thompson et al., 2006). One example of this concept is the interconnection of IPV *types* (e.g., physical and sexual violence) *together*. For example, a pilot study for the NISVS documented a higher number of total IPV types experienced among intimate partner stalking victims (3.4 types, on average) than sexual, physical, and psychological IPV victims (on average, 3.0 types, 2.5 types, and 1.9 types, respectively; Krebs et al., 2011). However, types are not the only IPV dimensions that intersect. The intersection of quantity and frequency of abuse plagues IPV victims at a rate of 26.2 percent, specifically when looking at multiple rounds of victimization by intimate partners; that is, 26.2 percent of IPV victims experience revictimization (Oudekerk & Truman, 2017). In terms of severity, 21.4 percent of women and 14.9 percent of men have experienced severe physical IPV at some point in their lifespan (see Smith et al., 2018). Dutton, Kaltman, Goodman,

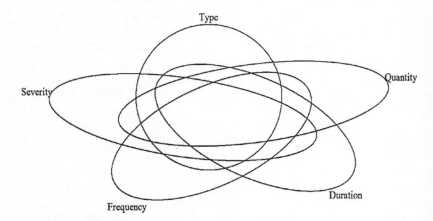

Figure 1.1 Depiction of intersecting dimensions of violence, abuse, and victimization.

Weinfurt, and Vankos (2005) found longer abuse duration in violent configurations of severe overlapping violence types than overlapping violence types of lesser severity.

Violence-perpetrating partners also use various harmful tools, as well as hybrid forms of abuse. For example, firearm violence constitutes a subsect of IPV that is particularly harmful and potentially lethal. In addition to firearms being used in 4.2 percent of all IPV victimizations, as well as in 4.7 percent of all female IPV victimizations (Catalano, 2013; Planty & Truman, 2013), over four million women have been threatened with a gun, with one million women shot or shot at (see Sorenson & Schut, 2018). Moreover, the presence of a firearm results in more than a 500 percent increase in the associated odds of transitioning from abuse to intimate femicide (Campbell et al., 2003). Non-fatal strangulation, what some researchers call a "hybrid" form of abuse (see Montanez et al., 2020) and a "live demonstration of power and control" (Pritchard, Reckdenwald, & Nordham, 2017, p. 407), tends to occur at higher rates toward women than men (see Mcquown et al., 2016; Sorenson, Joshi, & Sivitz, 2014; Stansfield & Williams, 2021). Additionally, according to multi-state research, 9.6 percent and 90.4 percent of intimate partner kidnappings include male and female victimization, respectively, leaving intimate partner kidnappings more gendered than non-intimate partner kidnappings (Blumenstein, 2015). Furthermore, relationships are contexts in which women are far more likely to be killed than men (see, e.g., Catalano, 2013; Fox & Fridel, 2017).

The Movement and the Criminal Legal System

While other points in the history brought attention to family violence, the most rigorous attempt to spotlight, understand, and eradicate IPV was grounded in the women's movement (Barner & Carney, 2011; Barnett, Miller-Perrin, & Perrin, 2011). Indeed, efforts and events spanning the late 19th and early 20th centuries, such as increased attention to women's subordinated status, the crystallization of the suffragist movement, and the ratification of the 19th Amendment, set the historical and attitudinal context that would make future IPV discussions possible (Barner & Carney, 2011; Barnett et al., 2011; Schechter, 1982).

In the 1960s, a reinvigorated feminist movement drove the fight for women's rights forward, further revealing women's experiences, including violence (Barnett et al., 2011). Developments in the late 1960s such as more open access to birth control and throughout the 1970s, which saw the creation of shelters for victims, created more rights, as well as spotlighted violence against women in the domesticsphere(Barner&Carney2011).Thiserafeaturedconsciousness-raising in which women started discussing with each other their hidden experiences of abuse in the home. Suddenly, individual women started rejecting self-blame because they realized they were not the only ones experiencing abuse; abuse started to be viewed as a widespread pattern of male perpetration (see Bailey, 2010; Schechter, 1982).

These dynamics set up the genesis of the shelter movement. A grassroots effort by women, including battered women themselves, drove the creation of shelters in many areas of the U.S. (see Bailey, 2010; Gondolf & Fisher, 1988; Pence & Paymar, 1993). However, in addition to the eventual professionalization of the movement (see Gondolf & Fisher, 1988), there has been a historical mistranslation between movement goals and criminal legal system processes and outcomes (Bailey, 2010).

Along these lines, the anti-violence movement has not progressed in a vacuum, meaning that other forces have been at play that have mitigated its effectiveness and reach in bringing relief to IPV victim-survivors of various backgrounds. For example, historically, the anti-violence movement developed against the backdrop of carceral forces and a dismantling of social programs for the economically disadvantaged (see Goodmark, 2018; Richie, 2012; for context, see Massey, 2007). While alternative framing of the story of the battered women's movement has been described (see Arnold & Ake, 2013), critical perspectives argue that the movement progressed with an "everywoman" analysis that did not fully consider racism and classism (see Richie, 2012), as well as with an "embrace of the criminalization agenda" (Goodmark, 2018, p. 12). The result has been an entrenched criminalization of IPV victim-survivors.

Immigration in the United States

In 2016, 43.7 million people in the U.S. were born outside of the country. The number of foreign-born persons in the U.S. has increased substantially since the 1960s. By 2065, the number of U.S. foreign-born persons is expected to exceed 78 million (López, Bialik, & Radford, 2018). A series of issues and features associated with immigration policy shape the experiences of persons who were/are born outside of the geographic borders of the U.S., such as detention, deportation, and family separation. For example, in the context of rising detention of immigrants across decades, federal policies, such as a 1996 law on "illegal immigration" that, among other things, expanded the reasons for which immigrants could be deported, have created a detention system in which jail-like conditions are the norm, interpersonal violence is ignored, and constitutional protections are not guaranteed. Indeed, an immigration system exists that overwhelmingly detains Latinx persons and is assisted by (and embedded in) a larger carceral system that triggers a pipeline to detention for Black migrants (see Saadi, Young, Patler, Estrada, & Venters, 2020). In 2018, the U.S. executive branch implemented a "zero tolerance" policy that, en masse, placed a barrier between migrant children and their parents. Continued separation of family units lingered after executive action canceling implementation of the policy (Kirbria, 2019). Indeed, although the U.S. immigration policy is historically a civil matter, the application of criminal matter force by the State without criminal matter protections renders the immigration system as a "crimmigration" system (see Kaufman, 2008; Patler & Golash-Boza, 2017; Ricciardelli, Nackerud, & Quinn, 2020).

Immigrants, Refugees, Intimate Partner Violence, Intersectionality, and Federal Policy

IPV cuts across various human experiences including race, class, disability, and sexual orientation. Interestingly, many IPV behaviors themselves, such as isolation and intimidation, mimic tactics used in systems of group domination and oppression (e.g., racism and ableism; Bancroft, 2002; Pence & Paymar, 1993). Grounded in the idea that analyses of sexism require simultaneous analyses of racism and vice-versa, *-isms* describing oppression crisscross each other to form context. In these contexts, people have experiences that are both derived from their separate component identities (e.g., based solely on being Black or based solely on being poor), as well as created based on their unique constellations of identity (e.g., unique to being a Black woman; see Crenshaw, 1989).

Intimate Partner Violence and Immigration

IPV affects persons who leave one country and rehome in another. Data from the 2010 NISVS show that experiencing intimate partner physical violence, contact sexual violence, and stalking at some point in the lifespan befell 37.3 percent of U.S. native women and 24 percent of foreign-born women—as well as 30.2 percent of U.S. native men and 17 percent of foreign-born men (Breiding et al., 2014). It is possible that these figures may not reflect "a true difference in prevalence," but rather "cultural differences in reporting" (p. 67). Moreover, it is also plausible that *some* immigrant victims, such as undocumented victims, may distrust research processes that request sensitive information. In the work by Njie-Carr et al. (2019), fear of being found by immigration officials induced fear in IMR women and decreased their willingness to provide contact information to researchers.

Stacked atop the complications that immigration status brings to immigrants and refugees, the inter-dimensional nature of violence stays present. For example, Hass, Dutton, and Orloff (2000) found that physical abuse infiltrated the lives of 49.3 percent of women in a sample of 280 Latina immigrants, with sexual abuse, dominance/isolation, and emotional/verbal abuse infiltrating the lives of 11.4 percent, 60 percent, and 40.7 percent of women, respectively.

Considerations regarding lethality reveal heightened risk for IMR victim-survivors of IPV. In a study on intimate partner homicide in New York City, being foreign-born was associated with an increase in the odds of intimate partner femicide by almost twofold (Frye, Hosein, Waltermaurer, Blaney, & Wilt, 2005). In the context of both homicides and homicide-suicides in multiple states within the U.S., an associated increase in the odds of foreign-born victims' deaths (as compared to U.S.-born victims) stemmed from IPV-related occurrences (Sabri, Campbell, & Messing, 2021).

IMR victim-survivors of IPV are not singular in their backgrounds and experiences. As shown in the U.S. Transgender Study, undocumented transgender immigrants experienced physical and/or sexual IPV at a rate of nearly 60 percent (James, Herman, Rankin, Keisling, Mottet, & Anafi, 2016; see also, Guadalupe-Diaz & West, 2020). Age, disability, and immigration status interlock to form compounding risk factors for IPV. For instance, a risk factor for IPV at the intersection of disability and immigration is low income; a risk factor for IPV at the age-immigration intersection is substance use of the violence-perpetrating partner; at the cross-section of disability, age, and immigration status are risk factors such as childhood victimization (Sasseville, Maurice, Montminy, Hassan, & St-Pierre, 2020).

Looking more closely into the realities of IPV in IMR lives uncovers compounding issues, such as family. In the lives of IMR victim-survivors, the family may be a salient entity when going through IPV for positive and negative reasons (Reina, Maldonado, & Lohman, 2013; Sabri et al., 2018; Ting, 2010). In general, family can be conducive to violence, while also providing support (e.g., financial; Reina et al., 2013; Sabri et al., 2018). For undocumented women, family forms a major part of (informal) networks that are relied upon heavily (Reina et al., 2013). For IMR women who survive IPV in general, children may catalyze survivors' perseverance to escape abuse and help mitigating suicidal ideation (Sabri et al., 2018).

Language is an often-discussed barrier for foreign-born victims who experience IPV (Akinsulure-Smith, Chu, Keatley, Rasmussen, 2013; Crenshaw, 1991; Menjívar & Salcido, 2002; Reina et al., 2013; Vidales, 2010). Language barriers can restrict understanding of available resources (Menjívar & Salcido, 2002), lessen access to shelters (Crenshaw, 1991), cause communication issues when contacting law enforcement, and maybe amplified by downward mobility associated with lack of available language training (Reina et al., 2013). But, once language in a host county is attained, it can help unlock the protective potential of help-seeking (Menjívar & Salcido, 2002).

Because of occurrences like these, anti-violence advocacy organizations often serve IMR populations. On one day in 2014, 19 percent of identified domestic violence programs in the U.S. provided "advocacy related to immigration" (National Network to End Domestic Violence [NNEDV], 2015). Subsequent repetitions of this one-day evaluation found that 18–22 percent of domestic violence programs provided immigration-related support and/or advocacy (see NNEDV 2016, 2017, 2018, 2019, 2020).

Federal Policy

Legal context is especially salient in victimization experiences of foreign-born persons. Indeed, foreign-born IPV victims worldwide often have an "irregular status"—as well as a status that may hinge on the presence of a male spouse (Menjívar & Salcido, 2002). While U.S. laws can provide enhanced freedom and hold violence-perpetrating partners accountable (see, e.g., Sabri et al., 2018), they may also be unhelpful or event detrimental (e.g., survivors not having "evidence" to support Battered Spouse Waiver applications; Crenshaw, 1991). Indeed, fear of deportation or outed immigration status recurs as a theme across works that explore the voices of IMR victim-survivors of IPV (see Crenshaw, 1991; Erez, Adelman, & Gregory, 2009; Reina et al., 2013; Sabri et al., 2018; Silva-Martinez, 2016; Vidales, 2010). Detention of IMR victim-survivors of IPV has been highlighted by media outlets in recent years (see, e.g., Jeltsen, 2018). A study of domestic violence calls in Los Angeles, California, showed that domestic violence call rates declined as awareness of immigration enforcement increased (Muchow & Amuedo-Dorantes, 2020). Thus, one can argue that in such cases, the idea of "walking on eggshells" (for an explanation of this phrase, see Davhana-Maselesele, 2011) can take on heightened meaning as certain victims are under surveillance by both the State *and* abusive partners (for more on the issue of deportation and the immigration legal system in general, see Chapter 4).

Coverture has been a feature of the U.S. immigration system. Historically, immigrant women who were victims of domestic violence, along with their immigration statuses and access to resources, were beholden to husbands. Immigrant women who were domestic violence victims had a painful dilemma: *stay* in the relationship and face revictimization; or, *escape* and risk other potential consequences including deportation (Erez & Harper, 2018).

Fortifying the potential for abusive partners' holds on battered immigrant women was a set of 1986 legislative outputs, the Marriage Fraud Amendments, aimed at curbing the use of fake marriages as a means to legal immigration status (see, e.g., 8 U.S.C. 1325[c]; see also Erez & Harper, 2018; Orloff & Kaguyutan, 2002). In 1990, the Battered Spouse or Child Waiver was passed, allowing for the omission of the conditional basis of permanent resident status in the case that a spouse or child was battered or subject to extreme cruelty (see 8 U.S.C. 1186a[c][4]; Orloff & Kaguyutan, 2002).

In 1994, the Violence Against Women Act (VAWA) provided legal mechanisms for immigrant domestic violence victim-survivors (Erez & Harper, 2018; Orloff & Kaguyutan, 2002). For example, the *VAWA self-petition* was created allowing victim-survivors to initiate their own petitions for legal status if they could prove, among other requirements, good moral character and the experience of battering or extreme cruelty (see 8 U.S.C. 1154[a][1][A], 2020; see also Erez & Harper, 2018; Orloff & Kaguyutan, 2002). Another 1994 legal mechanism, the *VAWA cancellation of removal* (8 U.S.C. 1229b, 2020), featured a victim-survivor's ability to request that their deportation be stopped (8 U.S.C. 1229b, 2020; Orloff & Kaguyutan, 2002).

Within the first decade of the 2000s, through the Victims of Trafficking and Violence Protection Act of 2000, the introduction of "U visas" synthesized two recourse mechanisms: perpetrator accountability and granting legal status to victims of criminal activity including domestic violence (see 8 U.S.C. 1101(a)(15)(u); 8 U.S.C. 1184; Erez & Harper, 2018; Orloff & Kaguyutan, 2002). In 2013, a reauthorization of VAWA broadened the U visa's coverage of violent behavior and expanded who could receive protection (i.e., children; Erez & Harper, 2018). Overall, while legal intervention has mitigated the potential for battered immigrant women to remain trapped in abusive relationships, limitations exist—such as (a) nuanced immigration policy outcomes across immigration statuses, (b) some victims' lacking key components of self-petition (e.g., marriage certificates), (c) distrust of law enforcement, and (d) enhanced "policing of immigration laws" (Erez & Harper, 2018, p. 460).

Federalism and Policy Development in the United States

In the U.S., the legal context surrounding IMR victim-survivors of IPV is nuanced by federalism. Overarching legal entities, which preside over individuals within their respective geographical boundaries, share sovereignty (Singh, 2003). First, there is an entity that has its own special powers that span the entire country. Second, there are 50 major sub-entities, each with its own legislative, executive, and judicial powers in relation to individuals bounded by its geography (Singh, 2003). These dynamics create variation in laws, policies, and regulations on IPV-related statutes concerning topics like healthcare (Willie, Stockman, Perler, & Kershaw, 2017), firearms (Zeoli et al., 2018), employment (Swanberg, Ojha, & Macke, 2012), and housing (National Housing Law Project, 2018). Moreover, "in apparent contradiction to federal supremacy over immigration control, many state governments are actively experimenting with immigration control policies" (Boushey & Luedtke, 2011, p. 392). However, seemingly missing from the extant discussion is an important intersection: state-level statutes targeting IPV in IMR lives.

Conclusion

IPV is a major social problem that is complicated by various factors including gender, multidimensionality, and the interplay between social movement and criminal legal system dynamics. Further complicating this social problem are the inequalities engrained in immigration status strata (e.g., being a permanent resident versus being undocumented). To disentangle the inequalities and hardships associated with the IPV–IMR intersection, federal policies such as the U-Visa have been implemented to provide protection from both violent partners and the State. Remaining unanswered from the extant literature is how the U.S.'s state-by-state mosaic complicates and interacts with federal policy and social inequalities to impact the status of IMR victim-survivors of IPV. So, moving forward into the contents of this book, the authors ask the following question: How do state-level statutes shape the status of IMR victim-survivors of IPV?

Note

1. Calculations made by the authors of the present research are based on figures from Smith et al. (2018).

References

8 U.S.C. 1101(a)(15)(U)

8 U.S.C. 1154(a)(1)(A)

8 U.S.C. 1184

8 U.S.C. 1186a(c)(4)

8 U.S.C. 1229b

8 U.S.C. 1325(c)

Akinsulure-Smith, A., Chu, T., Keatley, E., & Rasmussen, A. (2013). Intimate partner violence among West African immigrants. *Journal of Aggression, Maltreatment, & Trauma, 22*(2), 109–126.

Aratani, L. (2019, July 16). Trump's attack hits nerve for Americans also told to "go back to your country." *The Guardian*. Retrieved from https://www.theguardian.com/us-news/2019/jul/16/go-back-country-trump-racist-tweet-hit-nerve-americans

Arnold, G., & Ake, J. (2013). Reframing the narrative of the battered women's movement. *Violence Against Women, 19*(5), 557–578.

Bailey, K. D. (2010). Lost in translation: Domestic violence, "the personal is political," and the criminal justice system. *The Journal of Criminal Law and Criminology, 100*(4), 1255–1300.

Bancroft, L. (2002). *Why does he do that? Inside the minds of angry and controlling men.* New York, NY: The Berkley Publishing Group.

Barner, J. R., & Carney, M. M. (2011). Interventions for intimate partner violence: A historical review. *Journal of Family Violence, 26*(3), 235–244.

Barnett, O. W., Miller-Perrin, C. L., & Perrin, R. D. (2011). *Family violence across the lifespan: An introduction* (3rd ed). Thousand Oaks, CA: SAGE Publications, Inc.

Blumenstein, L. (2015). Exploratory study on intimate partner kidnapping. Is this a prevailing issue in intimate partner relationships. *Partner Abuse, 6*(4), 403–424.

Boushey, G., & Luedtke, A. (2011). Immigrants across the US federal laboratory: Explaining state-level innovation in immigration policy. *State Politics & Policy Quarterly, 11*(4), 390–414.

Breiding, M. J., Basile, K. C., Smith, S. G., Black, M. C., & Mahendra, R. (2015). *Intimate partner violence surveillance uniform definitions and recommended data elements, version 2.0.* Atlanta, GA: National Center for Injury Prevention and Control, Centers for Disease Control and Prevention.

Breiding, M. J., Chen, J., & Black, M. C. (2014). *Intimate partner violence in the United States – 2010.* Atlanta, GA: National Center for Injury Prevention and Control, Centers for Disease Control and Prevention.

Campbell, J. C., Webster, D., Koziol-McLain, J., Block, C., Campbell, D., Curry, M. A., ... & Laughon, K. (2003). Risk factors for femicide in abusive relationships: Results from a multisite case control study. *American Journal of Public Health*, *93*(7), 1089–1097.

Catalano, S. (2013, November). *Intimate partner violence: Attributes of victimization, 1993-2011*. U.S. Department of Justice, Office of Justice Programs, Bureau of Justice Statistics. Retrieved from https://bjs.ojp.gov/content/pub/pdf/ipvav9311.pdf

Crenshaw, K. (1989). Demarginalizing the intersection of race and sex: A Black feminist critique of antidiscrimination doctrine, feminist theory and antiracist politics. *University of Chicago Legal Forum*, 139–167.

Crenshaw, K. (1991). Mapping the margins: Intersectionality, identity politics, and violence against women of color. *Stanford Law Review*, *43*(6), 1241–1299.

Davhana-Maselesele, M. (2011). Trapped in a cycle of violence: A phenomenological study describing the stages of coping with domestic violence. *Journal of Social Science*, *29*(1), 1–8.

Davies, L., Ford-Gilboe, M., Willson, A., Varcoe, C., Wuest, J., Campbell, J., & Scott-Storey, K. (2015). Patterns of cumulative abuse among female survivors of intimate partner violence: Links to women's health and socioeconomic status. *Violence Against Women*, *21*(1), 30–48.

Dutton, M. A., Kaltman, S., Goodman, L. A., Weinfurt, K., & Vankos, N. (2005). Patterns of intimate partner violence: Correlates and outcomes. *Violence & Victims*, *20*(5), 483–497.

Erez, E., Adelman, M., & Gregory, C. (2009). Intersections of immigration and domestic violence: Voices of battered immigrant women. *Feminist Criminology*, *4*(1), 32–56.

Erez, E., & Harper, S. (2018). Intersectionality, immigration, and domestic violence. In R. Martínez, M. E. Hollis, & J. I. Stowell. *The handbook of race, ethnicity, crime, and justice*. Hoboken, NJ: John Wiley & Sons, Inc. (pp. 457–474).

Fox, A. F., & Fridel, E. E. (2017). Gender differences in patterns and trends in U.S. Homicide, 1976-2015. *Violence and Gender*, *4*(2), 37–43. doi: 10.1089/vio.2017.0016.

Gondolf, E. W., & Fisher, E. R. (1988). *Battered women as survivors: An alternative to treating learned helplessness*. New York, NY: Lexington Books.

Goodmark, L. (2018). *Decriminalizing domestic violence: A balanced policy approach to intimate partner violence*. Oakland, CA: University of California Press.

Guadalupe-Diaz, X., & West, C. M. (2020). The intersections of race and immigration. In A. M. Messinger, & X. Guadalupe-Diaz (Eds.), *Transgender intimate partner violence: A comprehensive introduction*. New York, NY: New York University Press.

Hamby, S., & Grych, J. (2013). *The web of violence: Exploring connections among different forms of interpersonal violence and abuse*. New York, NY: Springer.

Hass, G. A., Dutton, M. A., & Orloff, L. E. (2000). Lifetime prevalence of violence against Latina immigrants: Legal and policy implications. *International Review of Victimology*, *7*(1–3), 93–113.

James, S. E., Herman, J. L., Rankin, S., Keisling, M., Mottet, L., & Anafi, M. (2016). *The report of the 2015 U.S. transgender survey.* Washington, DC: National Center for Transgender Equality. Retrieved from https://transequality.org/sites/default/files/docs/usts/USTS-Full-Report-Dec17.pdf

Jeltsen, M. (2018, July 24). Domestic abusers have an ally in the Trump era. It's ICE. *Huffington Post.* Retrieved from https://www.huffpost.com/entry/ice-domestic-violence-abuse_n_5b561740e4b0b15aba914404

Johnson, M. P. (2008). *A typology of domestic violence: Intimate terrorism, violent resistance, and situational couple violence.* Boston, MA: Northeastern University Press.

Kaufman, M. (2008). Note: Detention, due process, and the right to counsel in removal proceedings. *Stanford Journal of Civil Rights and Civil Liberties, 4*, 113.

Kelly, U. A. (2011). Theories of intimate partner violence: From blaming the victim to acting against injustice: Intersectionality as an analytic framework. *Advances in Nursing Science, 34*(3), E29–E51.

Kelly, J. B., & Johnson, M. P. (2008). Differentiation among types of intimate partner violence: Research update and implications for interventions. *Family Court Review, 46*(3), 476–499.

Kirbria, N. (2019). #FamiliesBelongTogether: Facts and fictions of race and family in U.S. Immigration policy. *Sociological Forum, 34*(3), 809–817.

Krebs, C., Breiding, J. J., Browne, A., & Warner, T. (2011). The association between different types of intimate partner violence experienced by women. *Journal of Family Violence, 26*(6), 487–500.

Lax, J. R., & Phillips, J. H. (2009). Gay rights in the states: Public opinion and policy responsiveness. *American Political Science Review, 103*(3), 367–386.

López, G., Bialik, K., & Radford, J. (2018, November 30). Key findings about U.S. immigrants. *Pew Research Center.* Retrieved from http://www.pewresearch.org/fact-tank/2018/11/30/key-findings-about-u-s-immigrants/

Mcquown, C., Frey, J., Steer, S., Fletcher, G. E., Kinkopf, B., Fakler, M., & Prulhiere, V. (2016). Prevalence of strangulation in survivors of sexual assault and domestic violence. *The American Journal of Emergency Medicine, 34*(7), 1281–1285.

Menjívar, C., & Salcido, O. (2002). Immigrant women and domestic violence: Common experiences in different countries. *Gender & Society, 16*(6), 898–920.

Montanez, J., Donley, A., & Reckdenwald, A. (2020). Intersecting dimensions of violence, abuse and victimization. In H. Pontell (Ed.), *Oxford Research encyclopedia of criminology and criminal justice.* New York and Oxford: Oxford University Press. doi: 10.1093/acrefore/9780190264079.013.687

Morgan, R., & Oudekerk, B. A. (2019). *Criminal victimization, 2018.* U.S. Department of Justice, Office of Justice Program.

Muchow, A. N., & Amuedo-Dorantes, C. (2020). Immigration enforcement awareness and community engagement with police: Evidence from domestic violence calls in Los Angeles. *Journal of Urban Economics, 117*, 103253.

National Housing Law Project. (2018, July). *Housing rights of domestic violence survivors: A state and local law compendium.* Retrieved from https://www.nhlp.org/wp-content/uploads/2017-NHLP-DV-and-Hsing-State-Compendium-FINAL.pdf

National Network to End Domestic Violence. (2020). 14th annual domestic violence counts report. Retrieved from https://nnedv.org/wp-content/uploads/2020/03/Library_Census-2019_Report_web.pdf

National Network to End Domestic Violence. (2019). 13th annual domestic violence counts report. Retrieved from https://nnedv.org/wp-content/uploads/2020/03/Library_Census-2019_Report_web.pdf

National Network to End Domestic Violence. (2018). 12th annual domestic violence counts report. Retrieved from https://nnedv.org/wp-content/uploads/2019/07/Library_Census_2017_Report.pdf

National Network to End Domestic Violence. (2017). 11th annual domestic violence counts report. Retrieved from https://nnedv.org/wp-content/uploads/2019/07/Library_Census_2016_Report.pdf

National Network to End Domestic Violence. (2016). Domestic violence counts 2015. Washington, DC: National Network to End Domestic Violence, Inc.

National Network to End Domestic Violence. (2015). Domestic violence counts 2014. Retrieved from https://nnedv.org/wp-content/uploads/2020/04/Library_Census_2014_Full_Report.pdf

Njie-Carr, V. P. S., Sabri, B., Messing, J. T., Ward-Lasher, A., Johnson-Agbakwu, C. E., McKinley, C. ... Campbell, J. (2019). Methodological and ethical considerations in research with immigrant and refugee survivors of intimate partner violence. *Journal of Interpersonal Violence.* (Advance online publication).

Orloff, L. E., & Kaguyutan, J. V. (2002). Offering a helping hand: Legal protections for battered immigrant women: A history of legislative responses. *Gender, Social Policy, & the Law, 10*(1), 95–170.

Oudekerk, B. A., & Truman, J. L. (2017). *Repeat violent victimization, 2005-14.* U.S. Department of Justice, Office of Justice Programs, Bureau of Justice Statistics.

Patler, C., & Golash-Boza, T. M. (2017). The fiscal and human costs of immigrant detention and deportation in the United States. *Sociology Compass, 11.* doi: 10.1111/soc4.12536

Pence, E., & Paymar, M. (1993). *Education groups for men who batter: The Duluth model.* New York, NY: Springer Publishing Company, Inc.

Planty, M., & Truman, J. L. (2013). *Firearm Violence, 1993-2011.* U.S. Department of Justice, Office of Justice Programs, Bureau of Justice Statistics.

Pritchard, A. J., Reckdenwald, A., & Nordham, C. (2017). Strangulation as part of domestic violence: A review of research. *Trauma, Violence, & Abuse, 18*(4), 407–424.

Reina, A. S., Maldonado, M. M., & Lohman, B. J. (2013). Undocumented Latina networks and responses to domestic violence in a new immigrant gateway: Toward a place-specific analysis. *Violence Against Women, 19*(12), 1472–1497.

Ricciardelli, L. A., Nackerud, L., & Quinn, A. E. (2020). The criminalization of immigration and intellectual disability in the United States: A mixed methods approach to exploring forced exclusion. *Critical Social Work*, *21*(2), 19–40.

Richie, B. E. (2012). *Arrested justice: Black women, violence, and America's prison nation*. New York and London: New York University Press.

Saadi, A., Young, M., Patler, C., Estrada, J. L., & Venters, H. (2020). Understanding US immigration detention: Reaffirming rights and addressing social-structural determinants of health. *Health & Human Rights Journal*, *22*(1), 187–197.

Sabri, B., Campbell, J. C., & Messing, J. T. (2021). Intimate partner homicides in the United States, 2003-2013: A comparison of immigrants and nonimmigrant victims. *Journal of Interpersonal Violence*, *36*(9–10), 4735–4757.

Sabri, B., Nnawulezi, N., Njie-Carr, V. P. S., Messing, J., Ward-Lasher, A., Alvarez, C., & Campbell, J. C. (2018). Multilevel risk and protective factors for intimate partner violence among African, Asian, and Latina immigrant and refugee women: Perceptions of effective safety planning interventions. *Race and Social Problems*, *10*, 348–365.

Sasseville, N., Maurice, P., Montminy, L., Hassan, G., & St-Pierre, É. (2020). Cumulative contexts of vulnerability to intimate partner violence among women with disabilities, elderly women, and immigrant women: Prevalence, risk factors, explanatory theories, and prevention. *Trauma, Violence, & Abuse*, *23*(1), 88–100.

Schechter, S. (1982). *Women and male violence: The visions and struggles of the battered women's movement*. Boston, MA: South End Press.

Scott-Storey, K. (2011). Cumulative abuse: Do things add up? An evaluation of the conceptualization, operationalization, and methodological approaches in the study of the phenomenon of cumulative abuse. *Trauma, Violence, & Abuse*, *12*(3), 135–150.

Silva-Martínez, E. (2016). "El silencio": Conceptualizations of Latina immigrant survivors of intimate partner violence in the midwest of the United States. *Violence Against Women*, *22*(5), 523–544.

Singh, R. (2003). *American government and politics: A concise introduction*. Thousand Oaks, CA: SAGE Publications.

Smith, S. G., Zhang, X., Basile, K. C., Merrick, M. T., Wang, J., Kresnow, M., & Chen, J. (2018). *The national intimate partner and sexual violence survey (NISVS): 2015 data brief*. Atlanta, GA: National Center for Injury Prevention and Control, Centers for Disease Control and Prevention.

Sorenson, S. B., Joshi, M., & Sivitz, E. (2014). A systematic review of the epidemiology of nonfatal strangulation, a human rights and health concern. *American Journal of Public Health*, *104*, e54–e61. doi: 10.2105/AJPH.2014.302191

Sorenson, S., & Schut (2018). Nonfatal gun use in intimate partner violence: A systematic review of the literature. *Trauma, Violence, & Abuse*, *19*(4), 431–442.

Stansfield, R., & Williams, K. R. (2021). Coercive control between intimate partners: An application to nonfatal strangulation. *Journal of Interpersonal Violence*, *36*(9–10), NP5105–NP5124.

Straus, M. A., & Gelles, R. J. (1989). *Physical violence in American families: Risk factors and adaptations to violence in 8,145 families*. New Brunswick, NJ: Transaction.

Straus, M. A., Gelles, R. J., & Steinmetz, S. K. (1980/2006). *Behind closed doors: Violence in the American family*. New Brunswick, NJ: Transaction.

Swanberg, J. E., Ojha, M. U., & Macke, C. (2012). State employment protection statutes for victims of domestic violence: Public policy's response to domestic violence as an employment matter. *Journal of Interpersonal Violence, 27*(3), 587–619.

Thompson, R. S., Bonomi, A. E., Anderson, M., Reid, R. J., Dimer, J. A., Carrell, D., & Rivara, F. P. (2006). Intimate partner violence: Prevalence, types, and chronicity in adult women. *American Journal of Preventive Medicine, 30*(6), 447–457. doi: 10.1016/j.amepre.2006.01.016.

Tjaden, P., & Thoennes, N. (2000). *Extent, nature, and consequences of intimate partner violence: Findings from the national violence against women survey*. Washington, DC: National Institute of Justice.

Ting, L. (2010). Out of Africa: Coping strategies of African immigrant women survivors of intimate partner violence. *Health Care for Women International, 31*(4), 345–364.

Vidales, G. T. (2010). Arrested justice: The multifaceted plight of immigrant Latinas who faced domestic violence. *Journal of Family Violence, 25*, 533–544.

Zeoli, A. M., McCourt, A., Buggs, S., Frattaroli, S., Lilley, D., & Webster, D. W. (2018). Analysis of the strength of legal firearms restrictions for perpetrators of domestic violence and their associations with intimate partner homicide. *American Journal of Epidemiology, 187*(11), 2365–2371. doi: 10.1093/aje/kwy174

2 Methodology

This chapter introduces the methodology of the study, which drew inspiration from Crisafi (2016). The chapter begins by outlining the first stage of engaging in the act of searching for and compiling relevant statutes at the state level using the legal database of choice, *Nexis Uni*. Next, the second stage of compiling the statutes is discussed, which included checking the statutes mentioned within and located around the statutes found in the first stage. The chapter concludes by discussing steps regarding content analysis coding including the coding sheet and efforts undertaken to ensure intercoder reliability.

The Current Study

Search Strategy

In addition to a wide array of topics (e.g., IPV-inclusive Stand Your Ground law, IPV-related employment policies; see Crisafi, 2016; Swanberg, Ojha, & Macke, 2012, respectively), the extant academic literature has employed various methods to unearth statutes, laws, rules, and regulations across states which were considered in devising the present study. For example, some research has focused on statutes alone (Richards, Gover, & Tudor, 2018), while others have examined administrative regulations and statutes (Crisafi, 2016; Swanberg et al., 2012). To focus the scope of the study, we focused on statutes alone, excluding administrative regulations and website information. (Richards et al., 2018). To gauge the feasibility of searching for IMR-related IPV statutes, an initial *Google* search was first conducted in November 2018 using the terms "domestic violence" and "immigration," resulting in the discovery of Section 17b-112c of the Connecticut General Statutes and Section 402.87 of the Florida Statutes. In

DOI: 10.4324/9781003167044-2

December 2018, a broader convenience sample of statutes ($n = 4$) was compiled using the above search terms in *Google* to start to understand how these statutes are composed—as well as what components contributed to them. The statutes included:

- Cal Pen Code § 1463.27
- Conn. Gen. Stat. §17b-112c
- Fla. Stat. § 402.87
- Cal Pen Code § 13823.17

We used these statutes to grasp some characteristics that may be in other statutes as well as the type of terminology within them. The search for the universe of statutes related to IPV against IMR persons was conducted from February 2019 to June 2020.

For the main search, statutes in all 50 states and the District of Columbia (D.C.) were placed under inquiry. The present research includes all states/D.C., all statute types, and all effective dates to maximize inclusivity, comprehensiveness, and completeness.

Techniques used to compile multi-state policy lists include searching websites (see Holcomb et al., 2017; Richards et al., 2018; Swanberg et al., 2012) and law-related databases such as LexisNexis (see Crisafi, 206; Swanberg et al., 2012). Cross-referencing among keyword search terms has also been used in the literature (see Crisafi, 2016). To search for statutes, we used an adaptation of the search strategy conducted by Crisafi (2016), specifically the usage of search terms and cross-referencing within a legal database. Within Nexis Uni, we initiated an "exact phrase" search within the platform's "Advanced Search" function. Specifically, one of the various terms was within the exact phrase search—such as "domestic violence," "family violence," "domestic dispute," "battered," and "violence against women." We limited results to "Statutes and Legislation." Results were then further limited to "Codes." We then searched within the resulting list of statutes by entering one of the various terms—such as "immigrant," "alien," "refugee," and others. Thus, some examples of search terminology combinations are as follows: "immigrant" and "domestic violence"; "immigrant" and "family violence"; "domestic dispute" and "alien"; "domestic abuse" and "noncitizen"; and so on. The entirety of terms used in the search can be found in Table A.1 of the Appendix. The search strategy was performed from February 2019 to June 2020, though there was no limit to the inclusion of statutes based on the effective date.

It is common for policy researchers to note the limitations and barriers they face in attempting to capture the entire universe of state-level IPV-related statutes. For example, in an examination of workplace-related IPV statutes, it was noted that some statutes may have been "inaccessible using the methods used by the study's authors" (Swaberg et al., 2012, p. 612). To provide a "second line of defense" against such a limitation and come closer to capturing the entire universe of statutes related to IPV in IMR communities in the U.S., the initial statute search was followed by the following additional steps:

- For each statute found in the first stage, we searched through the five statutes preceding the original statute—as well as five statutes after the original statute (Stage Two).
- If a statute from the second stage was mentioned in another state-level statute, such a discovery was explored further.

The inclusion of statutes in the final list shown in the present research is based on the level of substantive content provided by the statute.[1] Accordingly, statutes mentioning only law titles and effective dates were excluded from the final list. The final list included 72 statutes and is presented in Table A.2 of the Appendix.

Measures

The coding scheme for the present research can be found in Table 2.1, which shows the variable names (e.g., relevant immigration terminology), categories within the variables (e.g., permanent resident, citizen), codes (e.g., "1," "0"), and meanings associated with codes (e.g., "1" equating to "Yes"). For example, within the variable "Human Trafficking" is a category asking whether a statute mentions human trafficking or trafficking in persons; two codes are provided, "1" and "0," which represent "Yes" and "No," respectively.

Construct Development

To develop coding categories described in Table 2.1, the first author developed an initial coding sheet based on readings of the convenience sample of statutes ($n = 4$) described earlier in this chapter. Throughout the search strategy, other terms and ideas became apparent and were integrated into the coding sheet accordingly. The first author added additional ideas and theories based on being exposed to further extant literature throughout the category development process.[2]

Table 2.1 Coding Scheme

Variable	Category	Code	Code Meaning
Immigration terminology considered[a]			
	Immigrant	1	Yes
		0	No
	Permanent resident	1	Yes
		0	No
	Refugee	1	Yes
		0	No
	PRUCL	1	Yes
		0	No
	Deeming	1	Yes
		0	No
	Nonimmigrant	1	Yes
		0	No
	Citizen	1	Yes
		0	No
	Noncitizen	1	Yes
		0	No
	Naturalization	1	Yes
		0	No
	Affidavit (of support)	1	Yes
		0	No
	Sponsor	1	Yes
		0	No
Subject/Domain[b]			
	Employment	1	Yes
	Health	2	Yes
	Housing	3	Yes
	Public benefits	4	Yes
	Law enforcement/CJ	5	Yes
	Voting	6	Yes
	Budgets	7	Yes
	Education	8	Yes
	Other	9	Yes
Human trafficking			
	Does the statute mention human trafficking or trafficking in persons?	1	Yes
		0	No
Federal Protection Components[c]			
	U-visa	1	Yes
		0	No
	T-visa	1	Yes
		0	No
	Self-petition	1	Yes
		0	No

(*Continued*)

Table 2.1 Coding Scheme (*Continued*)

Variable	Category	Code	Code Meaning
	Cancellation of removal	1	Yes
		0	No
	Asylum	1	Yes
		0	No
	Refugee status	1	Yes
		0	No
	Battered spouse or child waiver	1	Yes
		0	No
	Other	1	Yes
		0	No
Relevant issues[d]			
	Does the statute mention or address issues that commonly affect IMR victim-survivors of IPV?	1	Yes
		0	No
	Isolation	1	Yes
		0	No
	Economic dependence on partner	1	Yes
		0	No
	Language barrier	1	Yes
		0	No
	Gender norms	1	Yes
		0	No
	Other issues	1	Yes
		0	No
Resource shifting[e]			
	Does the statute shift resources?	1	Yes
		0	No
Demography[f]			
	Does the statute mention various demographic backgrounds?	1	Yes
		0	No
Victim[g]			
	Does the statute mention the term "victim"?	1	Yes
		0	No
Survivor[g]			
	Does the statute mention the term "survivor"?	1	Yes
		0	No
Resource creation[h]			
	Does the statute create a resource?	1	Yes
		0	No
Resource blocking			
	Are there aspects of the statute that block access to resources or protection?	1	Yes
		0	No

(*Continued*)

Table 2.1 Coding Scheme (*Continued*)

Variable	Category	Code	Code Meaning
Resource access[h]			
	Are there aspects of the statute that expand or streamline access to resources or protection?	1 0	Yes No
Surveillance/social control[i]			
	Is there an imposition of specific requirements that must be met by recipients of public benefits in order to maintain their eligibility for those benefits or protection?	1 0	Yes No

Notes: CJ = Criminal Justice; PRUCL = permanently residing under color of law.

a To offer as much focus on identities as possible, deviations from the aforementioned verbatim terms were not considered (e.g., *citizenship*, *immigration*). The terms were utilized in accordance with previous literature and the National Conference of State Legislatures (2018; see also Morse, 2018; Potochnick, Chen, & Perriera, 2017). Plural forms of the terms were also considered.

b Although statutes sometimes featured more than one of these subjects (for a discussion of subjects, see National Conference of State Legislatures, 2018), only one was coded based on discussion between the two coders regarding which subject was more pronounced within a statute.

c These were based on information from the Women's Law (n.d.) website. In addition to language and verbatim wording, statutes were also searched for statute code section numbers (e.g., *8 U.S.C 1101[a][15][U]* as an indicator of the U-visa).

d Careful consideration was given to context and meaning within the statute, such that the aforementioned issues were not conflated with related topics; for example, although a statute may have mentioned language as a topic, the statute may not have been classified as language barrier because it did not explicitly address difficulty accessing services, protection, etc. due to language.

e In coding shifts in resources, the coders focused on broader, institutional forms of resource displacement. For example, some of the statutes regarding protection orders in New York required alleged violence-perpetrating partners to return immigration-related documents to victims (see, e.g., NY CLS Fam Ct Act § 842, 2020). However, although a displacement (i.e., returning) of resources (i.e., documents) was ordered by the statute, the statute regarded the individual level and was thus not categorized as shifting resources.

f In addition to considering mention of specific demographics (e.g., women, transgender), the present research also included encompassing socio-demographic categories (e.g., race, nationality).

g To focus on identities, the term *victimization* was not considered. Plural versions of the terms, that is *survivors* and *victims*, were considered.

h Whereas the creation of a resource could technically be considered the expansion of a resource, the present research was coded in such a manner as to draw a distinction between the two constructs. Creation of a resource, as a construct, was based on whether a resource was non-existent before the adoption of the statute, whereas expansion/streamlining of a resource was based on already-existing resources.

i The methodology operationalized surveillance through the concept of social control (see Josephson, 2005).

Final Coding

Coding plans in the extant literature typically include qualitative and quantitative coding simultaneously. Swanberg et al. (2012) first segmented data into general themes, with a follow-up figuring of sub-themes. For Richards et al. (2018), "the coding … was created to represent the greatest variation possible in statutory language" (p. 9). For Crisafi (2016), "Quantitative and qualitative content analysis were used at every phase" (p. 88), and "a coding sheet was used to quantify" various characteristics "in each statute" (p. 82). Holcomb et al. (2017) also used "both qualitative and quantitative coding to track the collected data," while also recording the "data in a Microsoft Excel spreadsheet" (p. 421). Extant studies that analyze IPV-related laws, regulations, statutes, and rules tend to utilize multiple coders (see Holcomb et al., 2017; Richards et al., 2018; Swanberg et al., 2012). For example, Swanberg et al. (2012) utilized three coders, measuring the percentage of agreement between each coder and, after discussing and reexamining codes, reached a total agreement. Richards et al. (2018) calculated interclass calculations to measure inter-rater reliability among a subsample of statutes, finding optimal reliability across coders.

For final coding within the current research, the first and second authors placed various aspects of the statutes into categories using the spreadsheet processing program, Microsoft Excel. Categories (e.g., "immigrant," imposition of requirements) were placed in the spreadsheet as columns. The statute names were entered in the spreadsheet as rows. Codes (e.g., "1," "0," "Y") were entered at the intersections of appropriate columns and rows.

After both authors completed the coding, the resulting databases were compared and individual discrepancies in data points between the two coding databases were flagged. Within the spreadsheet, flagging of discrepancies was employed via the highlight function. The coders engaged in a discussion regarding such coding discrepancies to reach an agreement on final codes. These discussions occurred across three calls between the coders. Rules were constructed for categories to ensure that consistency was maintained in the discrepancy resolving process. At the end of the resolving process, a total agreement was reached.

After a total agreement was initially reached, the first author observed patterns in a particular variable (i.e., mention of various demographic backgrounds; see Chapter 3; see also Chapter 6). The patterns were organized into coding categories by the first author, into which both the first and second authors placed statutes separately. Further discrepancies between the resulting databases were flagged. Discussions were once again employed to reach full agreement on sub-codes. Total agreement was reached.

Display of Findings

To present data to the reader, many techniques exist within the literature. For example, in addition to quantifying and assigning scores to various characteristics, Richards et al. (2018) present a map to display variation across states. They also extract qualitative examples of statutes to show the reader important points. Swanberg et al. (2012) present their findings in the form of tables that indicate which, as well as the number of, states that possess certain statute themes. Holcomb et al. (2017) summarized the overall characteristics of FVO rules briefly in a table. Crisafi (2016) detailed each individual statute of interest. Following previous research, the present research employs many strategies to communicate findings: giving the percentage of statutes that fit within a particular category (see Swanberg et al., 2012), extracting qualitative examples to show the reader clear examples and variations of statutes (see Richards et al., 2018), summarizing some characteristics (where applicable) in the form of tables, and an overall map that shows which states have IMR IPV immigration statutes (see Richards et al., 2018 and, e.g., Figure A.1 of the Appendix).

Overall Theoretical and Empirical Strategy

The present research aims to emulate the quantitative explanatory framework with qualitative data. Just as many works using quantitative data aim to utilize various independent variables to explain dependent variables, the present research utilizes various theoretical frameworks as tools to dissect and explore state-level IMR-related IPV statutes to reach an answer to its overarching research question: How do state-level statutes in the U.S. shape the status of IMR persons who experience IPV (see Chapter 9)?

Conclusion

The current study analyzes 72 statutes that target IPV in IMR lives. Its beginnings were embodied in a search strategy and measurement/construct development. Deductive coding was employed (i.e., from theory to data) by two authors, with follow-up discussions purposed to resolve coding discrepancies and ensure intercoder reliability. Displaying findings in ways connected to the extant literature, the study aims to use multiple theoretical frameworks as tools to tell a story about what these statutes mean for the statuses of IMR victim-survivors of IPV.

Notes

1. During the search process, statutes on which the first author could not make a full determination on inclusion were sent to the second and third authors. All three authors discussed the statutes and commented on whether the questionable statutes should be included.
2. While many works code empirical characteristics (Crisafi, 2016; Holcomb et al., 2018; Swanberg et al., 2012), Richards et al. (2018) conceptually grounded their analysis in a broader framework. Specifically, they used the "Empowerment Process Model" as a theoretical ground for operationalizing the extent of victim participation in personal protection order processes across statutes.

References

Crisafi, D. (2016). *No ground to stand upon?: Exploring the legal, gender, and racial implications of stand your ground laws in cases of intimate partner violence*. Orlando, FL: University of Central Florida (Doctoral dissertation).

Holcomb, S., Johnson, L., Hetling, A., Postmus, J. L., Steiner, J., Braasch, L., & Riordan, A. (2017). Implementation of the family violence option 20 years later: A review of state welfare rules for domestic violence survivors. *Journal of Policy Practice, 16*(4), 415–431. doi: 10.1080/15588742.2017.1311820.

Josephson, J. (2005). The intersectionality of domestic violence and welfare in the lives of poor women. In N. J. Sokoloff, & C. Pratt (Eds.), *Domestic violence at the margins: Readings on class, gender, and culture*. New Brunswick, NJ: Rutgers University Press.

Morse, A. (2018, October 15). Common immigration terms. *National Conference of State Legislatures*. Retrieved from https://www.ncsl.org/research/immigration/common-immigration-terms.aspx

National Conference of State Legislatures. (2018, January). Report on state immigration laws: 2017. *Immigrant Policy Project*. Retrieved from https://www.ncsl.org/documents/immig/2017_Immigration_Report%20FINAL.pdf

Potochnick, S., Chen, J., & Perriera, K. (2017). Local-level immigration enforcement and food insecurity risk among immigrant families with children: National-level evidence. *Journal of Immigrant and Minority Health, 19*(5), 1042–1049.

Richards, T. N., Gover, A. R., & Tudor, A. (2018). A nation-wide assessment of empowerment among states' personal protective order statutes. *Journal of Interpersonal Violence* (Advance online publication). doi: 10.1177/0886260518794511.

Swanberg, J. E., Ojha, M. U., & Macke, C. (2012). State employment protection statutes for victims of domestic violence: Public policy's response to domestic violence as an employment matter. *Journal of Interpersonal Violence, 27*(3), 587–619.

Women's Law. (n.d.). *Legal Information: Federal: Immigration.* Retrieved from https://www.womenslaw.org/laws/federal/immigration/all

3   State Statutes, Identity, and Federal Policy

Introduction

This chapter describes the various aspects of IMR-related IPV statutes. This includes components such as whether they mention human trafficking, their connections with federal policy, and the possible inclusion of various identities. In addition to the geography and timing of statutes, the chapter looks at topics such as the U-visa, self-petition, and cancellation of removal.

States, Regions, Effective Dates, and Subjects

Seventeen states had IMR-related IPV statutes in effect (see Figure A.1 of the Appendix). Table 3.1 presents the percentage and number of statutes per state. California had the highest number of statutes. Illinois had the second highest quantity of statutes. Most of the IMR-related IPV statutes were present in the West (34.72 percent; $n = 25$), followed by the Northeast (30.55 percent; $n = 22$), Midwest (22.22 percent; $n = 16$), and South (12.5 percent; $n = 9$). The median number of statutes (across states with at least one statute) was three.

Timing

Table A.3 of the Appendix shows the effective dates of IPV-immigration language within statutes (i.e., with percentages of statutes effective per year). It seems that, with the exception of the year 2016 (which featured an increase in number of effective statutes), state-level statutes generally took effect within zero to three years after each federal VAWA passage/authorization in 1994, 2000, 2005, and 2013.

DOI: 10.4324/9781003167044-3

Table 3.1 Percentage of Statutes per State and Region (*N* = 72)

State or Region	n	%
Alabama	2	2.78
Arkansas	1	1.39
California	19	26.39
Connecticut	5	6.94
Florida	3	4.17
Iowa	1	1.39
Illinois	9	12.50
Indiana	1	1.39
Massachusetts	4	5.56
Minnesota	4	5.56
New Jersey	6	8.33
Nevada	1	1.39
New York	7	9.72
South Carolina	2	2.78
Texas	1	1.39
Washington	5	6.94
Wisconsin	1	1.39
Midwest	16	22.22
Northeast	22	30.55
South	9	34.72
West	25	12.50

Subjects

Table 3.2 presents the subjects/topics of statutes. There were five major categories: public benefits, criminal justice/law enforcement, budgets, health, and an "other" category.

Table 3.2 Subject/Domain of Statutes (as well as Mentions of Human Trafficking) (*N* = 72)

Category	n	%
Employment	0	0.00
Health	4	5.56
Housing	0	0.00
Public Benefits	31	43.06
Law Enforcement/Criminal Justice	27	37.50
ID/Drivers Licensing	0	0.00
Voting	0	0.00
Budgets	8	11.11
Education	0	0.00
Other	2	2.78
Mentions Human Trafficking or Trafficking in Persons	26	36.11

Public Benefits

The most common type of statute primarily regarded public benefits (43.06 percent; $n = 31$). These statutes focused on specific areas such as eligibility for cash and food assistance, status verification for public benefits, work requirements, and access to elderly home care and community-based services. For example, Section 402.87 of the Florida Statutes states partly as follows:

> The Department of Children and Families shall establish a structure by which the department shall:
>
> 1   Provide services to immigrant survivors of human trafficking, domestic violence, and other serious crimes, during the interim period between the time the survivor applies for a visa and receives such visa from the United States Department of Homeland Security or receives certification from the United States Department of Health and Human Services.
> 2   Ensure that immigrant survivors of serious crimes are eligible to receive existing state and local benefits and services to the same extent that refugees receive those benefits and services.
> 3   Ensure that immigrant survivors of serious crimes have access to state-funded services that are equivalent to the federal programs that provide cash, medical services, and social service for refugees. (Fla. Stat. § 402.87)

Law Enforcement/Criminal Justice

Approximately 38 percent ($n = 27$) of statutes focused on the criminal legal system and law enforcement. For instance, statutes concerned specific topics such as crime victim certification, assisting children in juvenile court cases, law enforcement training and protocols, judicial staff training, immigration/anti-sanctuary enforcement, training for district attorneys and assistant district attorneys, protection orders, legislative findings, and other matters. For example, Florida law establishes federal-local immigration enforcement but allows for IMR individuals to not be subject to such enforcement techniques:

> A law enforcement agency shall use best efforts to support the enforcement of federal immigration law … This section does not require a state entity, local governmental entity, or law enforcement agency to provide a federal immigration agency with information

related to a victim of or a witness to a criminal offense if the victim or witness timely and in good faith responds to the entity's or agency's request for information and cooperation in the investigation or prosecution of the offense ... This section does not apply to any alien unlawfully present in the United States if he or she is or has been a necessary witness or victim of a crime of domestic violence, rape, sexual exploitation, sexual assault, murder, manslaughter, assault, battery, human trafficking, kidnapping, false imprisonment, involuntary servitude, fraud in foreign labor contracting, blackmail, extortion, or witness tampering.

(Fla. Stat. § 908.104)

South Carolina features a similar phenomenon, such that domestic violence shelters (in general) do not violate local extensions of federal immigration enforcement:

It is a felony for a person who has come to, entered, or remained in the United States in violation of law to allow themselves to be transported, moved, or attempted to be transported within the State or to solicit or conspire to be transported or moved within the State with intent to further the person's unlawful entry into the United States or avoiding apprehension or detection of the person's unlawful immigration status by state or federal authorities ... Shelter provided for strictly humanitarian purposes or provided under the Violence Against Women Act is not a violation of this section, so long as the shelter is not provided in furtherance of or in an attempt to conceal a person's illegal presence in the United States.

Budgets

Eleven percent ($n = 8$) of statutes were categorized as budget laws, specifically concerning the following topics: restitution, grant funding for agencies providing domestic violence services to the LGBT community, grant funds for immigration services/assistance, allocation of grant funding for domestic violence service programs, budgets and requirements for legal service agencies, monies for outreach citizens to prospective citizens, eligibility and grant funding and eligibility for outreach to assist prospective citizens, and transfer of monies to fund outreach to prospective citizens. For example, in general, Section 1463.27 of the California Penal Code creates the possibility of levying a fee against domestic violence perpetrators. The funds collected from the fee "shall be used to fund domestic violence prevention programs that focus on assisting immigrants, refugees, or persons who live in a rural community" (Cal Pen Code § 1463.27).

Health

Approximately six percent (*n* = 4) of statutes focused primarily on health. These health-related statutes regarded medical assistance access, required training on domestic violence for medical professionals, grant funding for trauma recovery centers, and regulation of the functioning of trauma recovery centers. For example, Section 256B.06 of the Minnesota Statutes mentions the following:

a   Eligibility for medical assistance is limited to citizens of the United States, qualified noncitizens as defined in this subdivision, and other persons residing lawfully in the United States. Citizens or nationals of the United States must cooperate in obtaining satisfactory documentary evidence of citizenship or nationality according to the requirements of the federal Deficit Reduction Act of 2005, Public Law 109-171.

b   "Qualified noncitizen" means a person who meets one of the following immigration criteria:

1   admitted for lawful permanent residence according to United States Code, title 8;
2   admitted to the United States as a refugee according to United States Code, title 8, section 1157;
3   granted asylum according to United States Code, title 8, section 1158;
4   granted withholding of deportation according to United States Code, title 8, section 1253(h);
5   paroled for a period of at least one year according to United States Code, title 8, section 1182(d)(5);
6   granted conditional entrant status according to United States Code, title 8, section 1153(a)(7);
7   determined to be a battered noncitizen by the United States Attorney General according to the Illegal Immigration Reform and Immigrant Responsibility Act of 1996, title V of the Omnibus Consolidated Appropriations Bill, Public Law 104-200;
8   is a child of a noncitizen determined to be a battered noncitizen by the United States Attorney General according to the Illegal Immigration Reform and Immigrant Responsibility Act of

1996, title V, of the Omnibus Consolidated Appropriations Bill, Public Law 104-200; or

9 determined to be a Cuban or Haitian entrant as defined in section 501(e) of Public Law 96-422, the Refugee Education Assistance Act of 1980. (Minn. Stat. § 256B.06, 2020)

Other Statute Subjects

Approximately three percent ($n = 2$) of statutes did not fit easily into any of the aforementioned categories (health, budgets, criminal justice/law enforcement, and public benefits). These statutes were placed in a category named "Other." For example, Section 1816 of the California Family Code requires training for evaluators (e.g., supervising counselors), including some time reserved for the IPV-immigration intersection:

Twelve hours of instruction, as approved by the Administrative Office of the Courts, shall include all of the following:

1 The appropriate structuring of the child custody evaluation process, including, but not limited to, all of the following:

   a Maximizing safety for clients, evaluators, and court personnel.
   b Maintaining objectivity.
   c Providing and gathering balanced information from the parties and controlling for bias.
   d Providing separate sessions at separate times as described in Section 3113.
   e Considering the impact of the evaluation report and recommendations with particular attention to the dynamics of domestic violence.

2 The relevant sections of local, state, and federal laws, rules, or regulations.
3 The range, availability, and applicability of domestic violence resources available to victims, including, but not limited to, all of the following:

   a Shelters for battered women.
   b Counseling, including drug and alcohol counseling.
   c Legal assistance.
   d Job training.
   e Parenting classes.
   f Resources for a victim who is an immigrant. (Cal Fam Code § 1816)

Human Trafficking

In 2019, the U.S. National Human Trafficking Hotline identified 11,500 situations of human trafficking and more than 22,000 human trafficking victims and survivors. Sex trafficking and labor trafficking were identified as befalling roughly 15,000 and 5,000 of these victims-survivors, respectively. About 1,000 of the 22,000 victim-survivors were identified as experiencing *both* sex and labor trafficking. Another roughly 2,000 victim-survivors experienced trafficking of a "not specified" type (Polaris Project, n.d.). These numbers are anticipated to account for a fraction of the actual prevalence of human trafficking in the U.S. (Polaris Project, n.d.).

In 2000, the U.S. enacted the Trafficking Victims Protection Act (TVPA), which hinges on the following purpose: "to combat trafficking in persons, a contemporary manifestation of slavery whose victims are predominantly women and children, to ensure just and effective punishment of traffickers, and to protect their victims" (see 22 U.S.C. 7101). The TVPA defines "severe forms of trafficking in persons" in the following way:

a   sex trafficking in which a commercial sex act is induced by force, fraud, or coercion, or in which the person induced to perform such act has not attained 18 years of age; or
b   the recruitment, harboring, transportation, provision, or obtaining of a person for labor or services, through the use of force, fraud, or coercion for the purpose of subjection to involuntary servitude, peonage, debt bondage, or slavery. (see 22 U.S.C. § 7102[11])

Victims-survivors of human trafficking hold various immigration statuses—such as citizenship, permanent residence, and foreign national status (Polaris Project, n.d.). Thirty-six percent ($n = 26$) of IMR-related IPV statutes mentioned human trafficking or trafficking in persons. For example, an excerpt from the Illinois Compiled Statutes states as follows:

a   Persons who are foreign-born victims of trafficking, torture, or other serious crimes and who are receiving cash assistance or SNAP benefits under this Article shall be subject to the same work requirements and work requirement exemptions as other recipients of cash assistance or SNAP benefits, provided that compliance with these requirements is authorized by law.

b   A person who is a foreign-born victim of trafficking, torture, or other serious crimes shall be exempted from any work requirements if physical or psychological trauma related to or arising from the trafficking, torture, or other serious crimes impedes his or her ability to comply. (305 ILCS 5/16-4)

Law, Identity, and Stigma

Identities

Humans experience other humans in various roles and situations that extend across space and time; for example, while a person throwing a ball at a baseball game may have a certain identity in that particular situation (i.e., pitcher), an identity that spans a broader time and space also exists (i.e., athlete). The latter, social identity, focuses on the identification with and belonging to communities, groups, and encompasses social categories in a way that allows humans to draw similarities and contrasts with each other (Hewitt & Shulman, 2011). Labels may signify social identities and associated characteristics.

In addition to reflecting cultural context, the law may underscore the significance of certain characteristics, continue inter-group distinctions, or problematize characteristics (Burris, 2002). As a more specific example, Rosa's Law, a federal legislative output affecting labor, education, and health policy, changed the stigmatizing term *mental retardation* to *intellectual disability* (see Ford, Acosta, & Sutcliffe, 2013; Friedman, 2016). Goffman (1963) defines the term *stigma* as "an attribute that is deeply discrediting" (p. 3). For victim-survivors of IPV, stigma can stem from various sources. With abuse as a starting point, victims may undergo a process of believing the "negative messages" that society engrains into how they see themselves (Murray & Crowe, 2017). The discrediting function of stigma becomes salient in victims not being believed or actually being blamed, such as family/friends' believing that victims-survivors wait too long to voice their experiences (see Murray & Crowe, 2017). Moreover, the meanings behind identity labels—such as the term *battered immigrant*—can vary from context to context (i.e., public policy to community organizing to socio-political rights discourse; see Bhuyan, 2008).

Immigration Terms

The statutes within the present research featured a number of labels that represent immigrant and refugee identities, as well as victimization

36   *State Statutes, Identity, and Federal Policy*

Table 3.3 Immigration-Related and Victimization-Related Terminology within Statutes (*N* = 72)

Terminology	n	%
Immigration Terms		
Immigrant	24	33.33
Alien	12	16.67
Permanent Resident	18	25.00
Refugee	17	23.61
Permanently Residing Under Color of Law	4	5.56
Deeming	6	8.33
Nonimmigrant	10	13.89
Citizen	15	20.83
Noncitizen	14	18.06
Naturalization	2	2.78
Affidavit (of Support)	4	5.56
Sponsor	8	11.11
Victimization Terms		
Victim	44	61.11
Survivor	3	4.17

terms. Table 3.3 presents these terms' prevalence within the statutes. For example, the term *immigrant* was utilized in about 33 percent (*n* = 24) of the statutes. The term *refugee* was utilized in about 25 percent (*n* = 18) of statutes. About 21 (*n* = 15) percent of statutes included the term *citizen*.

Statutes decorated the aforementioned terms with various descriptors. For example, decorating the term *immigrant* were terms such as *unauthorized* and *lawfully residing*. Describing the term alien were words such as *lawfully present, lawfully residing immigrant, qualified, unlawfully present, conditional resident, eligible, legal, illegal, not eligible*, and *other*. In a more specific example, describing the parameters of eligibility for the New Jersey Work First Program, Section 44:10-48 of the New Jersey Revised Statutes states (partly) as follows:

… The following persons shall not be eligible for assistance and shall not be considered to be members of an assistance unit:

1   non-needy caretakers, except that the eligibility of a dependent child shall not be affected by the income or resources of a non-needy caretaker;
2   Supplemental Security Income recipients, except for the purposes of receiving emergency assistance benefits pursuant to section 8 of P.L.1997, c.14 (C.44:10-51);
3   illegal aliens;

4   other aliens who are not eligible aliens;
5   a person absent from the home who is incarcerated in a
     federal, State, county or local corrective facility or under the
     custody of correctional authorities, except as provided by reg-
     ulation of the commissioner ... (N.J. Stat. § 44:10-48)

Victimization Terms

Approximately 61 percent ($n = 44$) of statutes mentioned the term
victim. Four percent ($n = 3$) of statutes mentioned the term *survivor*
(see Table 3.3). Cross-tabulating IMR identities with IPV identities
showed that, among statutes mentioning the term *survivor*, there were
no references to the terms *alien, permanent resident, PRUCL, citizen,
noncitizen*, or *sponsor* (see Table 3.4).

The Federal-State Policy Connection

State-level statutes mentioned various extant federal level policies,
such as the Battered Spouse or Child Waiver, VAWA Self-Petition, and
the U-Visa (see Table 3.5).

Battered Spouse or Child Waiver

Section 1325(c) of Chapter 8 of the U.S. Code levies a criminal penalty
for using marriage to purposely defraud immigration law. The federal

Table 3.4 Cross-tabulations of Immigration and Victimization Identities
($N = 72$)

| | | | Victimization Identity Terms | | | |
| | Total | | Victim | | Survivor | |
Immigration Identity Terms	*n*	*%*	*n*	*%*	*n*	*%*
Alien	12	16.67	7	9.72	0	0.00
Citizen	15	20.83	7	9.72	0	0.00
Immigrant	24	33.33	16	22.22	3	4.17
Noncitizen	13	18.06	11	15.28	0	0.00
Nonimmigrant	10	13.89	9	12.50	1	1.39
Permanent Resident	18	25.00	7	9.72	0	0.00
PRUCL	4	5.56	3	4.17	0	0.00
Sponsor	8	11.11	7	9.72	0	0.00

Note: PRUCL = Permanently Residing Under Color of Law. All percentages are based on
$N = 72$. Three statutes mentioned "Survivor." Forty-four statutes mentioned "Victim."

Table 3.5 Federal Protection Components Mentioned
within Statutes ($N = 72$)

Federal Protection Component	n	%
U-Visa	15	20.83
T-Visa	13	18.06
Self-Petition	4	5.56
Cancellation of Removal	2	2.78
Asylum	13	18.06
Refugee Status	13	18.06
Battered Spouse or Child Waiver	7	9.72
Other	7	9.72

statute, one of the Marriage Fraud Amendments of 1986, states the
following:

> Any individual who knowingly enters into a marriage for the
> purpose of evading any provision of the immigration laws shall
> be imprisoned for not more than 5 years, or fived not more than
> $250,000, or both. (8 U.S.C. § 1325[c])

In 1990, the first IPV-immigration federal protection mechanism
came into existence: the Battered Spouse or Child Waiver (Orloff &
Kaguyutan, 2002). A piece of the Battered Spouse Waiver puts forth
the that the "condition basis of permanent resident status" may be
removed in instances in which a person (a) formed marriage in good
faith, (b) experienced battering/extreme cruelty by the spouse, and (c)
would experience "extreme hardship" if subject to removal (8 U.S.C.
§ 1186a[c][4]).

One statute mentioned language that approximated the language of
the Battered Spouse or Child Waiver, making reference to the Federal
Register:

> A person who meets the conditions of eligibility … and who meets
> either of the following requirements shall be eligible for partici-
> pation in the family investment program …The person is a con-
> ditional resident alien who was battered or subjected to extreme
> cruelty, or whose child was battered or subjected to extreme cru-
> elty, perpetrated by the person's spouse who is a United States
> citizen or lawful permanent resident as described in 8 C.F.R.
> §216.5(a)(3) …
>
> (see Iowa Code § 239B.2B)

VAWA Self-Petition

In the U.S. IMR victim-survivors of IPV have the option to, for themselves, submit an application to petition for immigration status (Erez & Harper, 2018; Orloff & Kaguyutan, 2002). This remedy–the VAWA self-petition–is legally textualized within Section 1154(a)(1)(A) of Chapter 8 of the U.S. Code, which reads as follows:

> An alien who ... may file a petition with the Attorney General under this clause for classification of the alien (and any child of the alien) if the alien demonstrates to the Attorney General that- ... the marriage or the intent to marry the United States citizen was entered into in good faith by the alien; and ... during the marriage or relationship intended by the alien to be legally a marriage, the alien or a child of the alien has been battered or has been the subject of extreme cruelty perpetrated by the alien's spouse or intended spouse ... an alien described in this subclause is an alien- ... who is the spouse of a citizen of the United States; ... who believed that he or she had married a citizen of the United States and with whom a marriage ceremony was actually performed and who otherwise meets any applicable requirements under this chapter to establish the existence of and bona fides of a marriage, but whose marriage is not legitimate solely because of the bigamy of such citizen of the United States; or ... who was a bona fide spouse of a United States citizen within the past 2 years and- ... whose spouse died within the past 2 years; ... whose spouse lost or renounced citizenship status within the past 2 years related to an incident of domestic violence; or ... who demonstrates a connection between the legal termination of the marriage within the past 2 years and battering or extreme cruelty by the United States citizen spouse; ... who is a person of good moral character; ... who is eligible to be classified as an immediate relative under ... this title or who would have been so classified but for the bigamy of the citizen of the United States that the alien intended to marry; ... who has resided with the alien's spouse or intended spouse.
>
> (8 U.S.C. § 1154(a)(1)(A))

In the present research, four statutes (5 percent) mentioned self-petition in some way. For example, section 10609.97 of the California Welfare and Institutions Code, which focuses on sharing information publicly for the benefit of IMR youth, reads partly as follows:

The State Department of Social Services shall provide guidance on best practices and facilitate an exchange of information and best practices among counties on an annual basis, commencing no later than January 1, 2014, on assisting a child in a juvenile court case who is eligible for special immigrant juvenile status under Section 1101(a)(27)(J) of Title 8 of the United States Code. This exchange of information may be accomplished by posting training and other information on the department's Internet Web site ... The guidance shall include procedures for assisting eligible children in applying for special immigrant juvenile status, before the children reach 21 years of age or get married, and applying for T visas, U visas, and Violence Against Women Act self-petitions.
(Cal Wel. & Inst. Code § 10609.97)

Two of the four statutes focused on criminal justice as a subject/ domain; one statute focused on budgets; one statute focused on law enforcement and criminal justice.

U-Visa

The U-visa is a mechanism that provides protection to victim-survivors of abuse (e.g., domestic violence) who have the potential of being helpful in the investigation/prosecution of such abuse-related criminal activity (8 U.S.C. 1101[a][15][U]). The petition associated with this protection is required to include certification by certain officials (e.g., prosecutors) attesting to the victim-survivor's (potential) helpfulness (8 U.S.C. § 1184[p]).

According to the U.S. Department of the State report, from 2015 to 2019 there were 651 nonimmigrant visas issued based on classification as "victim of criminal activity" (Table XVI[B], n.d.). There are also nonimmigrant visas that are issued based on proximity to a victim of criminal activity. From 2015 to 2019, there were 699 nonimmigrant visas issued based on the classification of being a spouse of a victim of criminal activity. Well over 6,000 nonimmigrant visas were issued to those classified as children of victims of criminal activity. One hundred eighty-one nonimmigrant visas were issued to those classified as parents of victims of criminal activity under 21 years of age. Finally, there were 197 nonimmigrant visas issued to those classified as unmarried siblings under age 18 of victims of criminal activity under 1 year of age (Table XVI[B], n.d.).

Twenty-one percent ($n = 15$) of statutes within the present research discussed, in some way, the U-visa or U nonimmigrant status. Some of these statutes dealt directly with crime victim certification. Others focused on public benefits. For some statutes, the U-visa was included as a topic in law enforcement, social services, and judicial staff training.

T-Visa

Eighteen percent (*n* = 13) of statutes were coded as mentioning the T-visa. The T-visa is a mechanism that provides protection to victim-survivors of severe human trafficking who comply with "reasonable request for assistance" for the investigation/prosecution of trafficking or trafficking-related crime (8 U.S.C. § 1101[a][15][T]). The basis of trafficking in persons is based on "severe forms of trafficking in persons" (see "Human Trafficking" section in Chapter 3).

According to the U.S. Department of the State report, from 2015 to 2019 there were zero visas classified as "T1," or "Victim of severe form of trafficking in persons." There are also nonimmigrant visas that are issued based on proximity to such victims. From 2015 to 2019 there were 457 nonimmigrant visas issued based on the classification of "T2," that is, spouse of a victim of a severe form of trafficking in persons. Over 1,600 visas were issued to those classified under "T3," or child of victim of a severe form of trafficking in persons. Ninety-nine vias were issued to those categorized as "T4," or Parent of a victim of a severe form of trafficking in person under 21 years of age. "T5" visas–those regarding unmarried siblings under age 18 of a victim of a severe form of trafficking in persons under 21 years of age–were issued 120 times. Nearly 40 visas of "T6" classification were issued: adult/minor child of derivative beneficiary of victim of a severe form of trafficking in persons (Table XVI[B], n.d.).

Cancellation of Removal

About three percent (*n* = 2) of statutes mentioned cancellation of removal, specifically by mentioning the mechanism in the context of budgets and public benefits. Cancellation of removal is a legal mechanism by which deportation/removal can be stopped. The U.S. Code has a special provision for "battered spouse[s] or child[ren]," which allows cancellation of removal in light of certain conditions:

- experiences of battering or "extreme cruelty" by a citizen or LPR spouse or intended spouse;
- three years of continuous physical presence in the U.S.;
- good moral character;

- admissible; and
- under threat of extreme hardship if removal occurs.

In this context, the status of the person would be adjusted from deportable to lawful (see 8 U.S.C. § 1229b).

Refugee Status

Eighteen percent (*n* =13) of statutes were coded as mentioning refugee status, in which the U.S. may admit persons who are stateless, of "special humanitarian concern," and admissible (8 U.S.C. § 1157). According to Section 1101(a)(42)(A) of Title Eight of the U.S. Code, a refugee is someone physically located external to the U.S. who has experienced fear of persecution based on one or more of several statuses (e.g., religion, race). In Section 13283 of the California Welfare and Institutions Code, California uses benefits for refugees as a benchmark for determining benefit standards for IMR victim-survivors of IPV:

> Notwithstanding any other provision of law, the department shall ensure that noncitizen victims of trafficking, domestic violence, and other serious crimes, as defined in subdivision (b) of Section 18945, have access to refugee cash assistance, and refugee employment social services set forth in this chapter, to the same extent as individuals who are admitted to the United States as refugees under Section 1157 of Title 8 of the United States Code. These individuals shall be subject to the same work requirements and exemptions as other participants, provided that compliance with these requirements is authorized by law. An exemption from these requirements shall be available if physical or psychological trauma related to or arising from the victimization impedes their ability to comply. Assistance and services under this subdivision shall be paid from state funds to the extent federal funding is unavailable.
>
> (Cal Wel & Inst Code § 13283)

Asylum

Asylum is a legal mechanism that provides protection from removal, authorization to work, and the possibility of being able to travel abroad to persons in the U.S.'s interior who have experienced fear of persecution based on one or more of several statuses (e.g., religion, race). Approximately 18 percent (*n* = 13) of state-level statutes mentioned or alluded to asylum. These statutes concerned public benefits (SNAP, TANF) but also concerned budgeting and requirements for nonprofit legal services/agencies.

> To the extent not otherwise provided in this Code or federal law, all clients who receive cash or medical assistance ... must meet the citizenship requirements as established in this Section. To be eligible for assistance an individual, who is otherwise eligible, must be either a United States citizen or included in one of the following categories of non-citizens ... (3) Asylees under Section 208 of the Immigration and Nationality Act ...
>
> (305 ILCS § 5/1-11)

Other Policy Components

State-level statutes discussed other protection components as well. About ten percent (*n* = 7) of statutes were coded as representing this category. For example, in discussing grant funding for immigration services/assistance, Section 13303 of the California Welfare and Institutions discusses Deferred Action for Childhood Arrivals (DACA) alongside IPV-related federal protection components:

a   Subject to the availability of funding in the act that added this section or the annual Budget Act, the department shall provide grants, as described in subdivision (b), to organizations qualified under Section 13304.

b   Grants provided in accordance with subdivision (a) shall be for the purpose of providing one or more of the following services, as determined by the department:

   1   Services to persons residing in, or formerly residing in, California, including, but not limited to, any of the following:

      a   Services to assist with the application process for initial or renewal requests of deferred action under the DACA policy with the United States Citizenship and Immigration Services.

      b   Services to obtain other immigration remedies.

      c   Services to assist with the naturalization process and any appeals arising from the process.

The statute goes on to discuss both DACA and "immigration remedies":

1   "DACA" refers to Deferred Action for Childhood Arrivals status as described in guidelines issued by the United States Department of Homeland Security... (4) "Immigration remedies" include, but shall not be limited to, U-visas, T-visas, special immigrant juvenile status, Violence Against Women Act self-petitions, family-based petitions, cancellation of removal, and asylum, or other remedies that may also include remedies necessary to enable pursuit of immigration protections. (Cal Wel & Inst. Code § 13303)

DACA, defined broadly as "a formal status that acts as a temporary reprieve and stays deportations" (Olivas, 2020, p. 13), had its historical and inspirational grounds in the proposed federal Development, Relief, and Education for Alien Minors (DREAM) Act and its various state-level versions. Brought forth in the U.S. in 2001, the DREAM Act was introduced in multiple legislative sessions. In its 2009–2010 form, the legislation aimed to "permit States to determine State residency for higher education purposes and to authorize the cancellation of removal and adjustment of status of certain alien students who are long-term United States residents and who entered the United States as children, and for other purposes." (p. 39). While the legislation ultimately failed to make it through Congress (i.e., failing the motion to invoke cloture in the Senate), it served as DACA's "closest precursor" (p. 39). DACA was implemented by the 44th U.S. president in 2012. "deferred deportation for renewable two-year periods" and provided mechanisms like "lawful presence" (Olivas, 2020, pp. 64–65).

Statutes also discussed special immigrant juvenile status. For example, in discussing budgeting and requirements for nonprofit legal services/agencies, Section 13301 of the California Welfare and Institutions Code partly states as follows:

Contracts awarded pursuant to Section 13300 shall fulfill all of the following:

a   Be executed only with nonprofit legal services organizations that meet all of the following requirements:

1   Have at least three years of experience handling asylum, T-Visa, U-Visa, or special immigrant juvenile status cases and have represented at least 25 individuals in these matters.

2   Have experience in representing individuals in removal proceedings and asylum applications.

3   Have conducted trainings on these issues for practitioners beyond their staff.
4   Have experience guiding and supervising the work of
attorneys whom themselves do not regularly participate
in this area of the law but nevertheless work pro bono on
the types of cases described in paragraph (1).
5   Are accredited by the Board of Immigration Appeals
under the United States Department of Justice's Executive
Office for Immigration Review or meet the requirements
to receive funding from the Trust Fund Program admin-
istered by the State Bar of California.

Special immigrant juvenile status is a mechanism by which harmed,
undocumented children may obtain immigration relief (see 8 U.S.C.
§ 1101[a][27][J]; see also Reynolds, 2021).

Discussion

This chapter looked at various empirical characteristics of IMR-
related IPV statutes. It engaged in an analysis that spotlighted geography, time, public benefits, criminal justice, health, budgets, human
trafficking, identity terms, and the federal-state policy connection.
Discussed below are some connection points to previous literature
based on findings that may be salient in the lives of IMR victim-
survivors of IPV.

Human Trafficking

Over one-third of statutes mentioned, in some form, human trafffick-
ing. This finding is particularly salient due to "similarities" between
persons who perpetrate IPV and persons who perpetrate trafficking
(Koegler, Howland, Gibbons, Teti, & Hanni, 2020). One study cen-
tered in the Midwestern U.S. found that over half of human trafficking
cases in the domestic setting featured a trafficker who was the victim's
intimate partner (Koegler et al., 2020).

Immigration Terminologies

Statuses conferred by the immigration legal system may be important
in the lives of IMR victim-survivors of IPV. For example, six statutes
juxtaposed the term *citizen* with the term *noncitizen*. Seven statutes
juxtaposed the term *citizen* with the term *alien*. In these statutes,

the line between statuses is drawn clearly within the text. This line between a status with more rights and status with lesser rights has been found in the extant literature, in which an asymmetrical social power dynamic is created in violent relationships based on immigration status (e.g., a dyad featuring a U.S. citizen and a person who is undocumented; see Akinsulure-Smith, Chu, Keatley, & Rasmussen, 2013; Erez, Adelman, & Gregory, 2009).

Victimization Terminologies, Structure, Movements, Stigma, and Legal Operationalization

Across statutes, the term *victim* was used with greater frequency than the term *survivor*. This finding is important because the frequencies at which they are used in the legal text give a hint to the structural, movement, and institutional dynamics that underpin legal operationalization in relation to stigma. While both terms represent people who experience violence, the *victim* seems to have a more negative, passive, and stigmatized connotation (Leisenring, 2006; Murray & Crowe, 2017). On the other hand, the term *survivor* has a more positive connotation, is associated with agency, and is less stigmatizing (Leisenring, 2006; Murray & Crowe, 2017).

Typifications of people who experience IPV have been deemed useful for promoting the need for policies and practices that help such individuals. Social movements may frame people who experience IPV in certain ways to appeal to emotions that resonate with the encompassing culture; for example, victim typification(s) draw on blamelessness to trigger sympathy so that the issue at hand is taken more seriously. These typifications can be stigmatizing because they run counter to individualism's emphasis on personal responsibility (Dunn, 2004). Sometimes typifications that aim to help are violated; thus, vocabularies of motive are produced to mitigate the stigma associated with the deviance of violating such typifications (Dunn, 2005). For example, people who experience IPV and make the decision to stay in a violent relationship violate the blamelessness norm in the eyes of the public because a particular level of violence should trigger a flight from the situation (Dunn, 2005). To account for these violations and deflect responsibility from people who experience abuse, themes like fear, guilt, structural barriers appealed to emotion to show that victims were entrapped. At the same time, themes associated with victim typifications are stigmatizing. Over time, survivor typifications emerged, painting people who experience IPV as having a more forward directionality (e.g., agency), such that staying/leaving/returning become survival tactics (Dunn, 2005).

Thus, a potential explanation for the asymmetric usage of the terms *victim* and *survivor* across IMR-related IPV statutes is that the term *victim* is one that, while to an extent stigmatizing, frames people who experience IPV as blameless and needing help from the State. On the other hand, the term *survivor* may be so indicative of agency that people who experience IPV may seem too self-sufficient for State help. Moreover, there is a time disconnect between movement dynamics and legal operationalization. That is, there is a lag in which institutionalization of ideas into state-level laws follows behind activism. Since victim typifications seem to have materialized first and then shifted toward survivor typifications within movement activism (Dunn, 2005), it is possible that the legal system is still taking its time to codify victim typifications and has yet to codify survivor typifications, resulting in the *victim/survivor* terminological asymmetry within statutes. One idea worth noting is the impact of individualism (and the notion of personal responsibility) on the shaping of victim and survivor typifications in relation to the state. These IMR-related IPV statutes are sites in which oppressive and anti-discrimination forces spar over immigration control, public benefit control, and criminalization (see Chapter 10). Accordingly, it is possible that etching the term *victim* into statutes was one of the ways to activate blamelessness and sympathy for IMR persons experiencing IPV in a political context that emphasized "personal responsibility" and heavily stigmatized IMR identities and statuses.

Conclusion

This chapter looked at the descriptive characteristics of IMR-related IPV statutes at the state level in the U.S. The contents covered geographic and temporal aspects of the statutes: respective states, geographies, and effective dates. The chapter also covered topics/subjects of the states, as well as whether they mentioned human trafficking or trafficking in persons. Immigration and victimization identities, as well as their cross-sections and implications of stigma, were also covered. Finally, the contents of the chapter looked at the state-level mention of federal protection components.

References

Akinsulure-Smith, A. M., Chu, T., Keatley, E., & Rasmussen, A. (2013). Intimate partner violence among West African immigrants. *Journal of Aggression, Maltreatment, & Trauma, 22*(1), 109–129.

Burris, S. (2002). Disease stigma in U.S. Public health law. *Journal of Law, Medicine, & Ethics, 30*, 179–190.

Bhuyan, R. (2008). The production of the "battered immigrant" in public policy and domestic violence advocacy. *Journal of Interpersonal Violence*, *23*(2), 153–170.

Dunn, J. (2004). The politics of empathy: Social movements and victim repertoires. *Sociological Focus*, *37*(3), 235–250.

Dunn, J. (2005). "Victims" and "survivors": Emerging vocabularies of motive for "battered women who stay. *Sociological Inquiry*, *75*(1), 1–30.

Erez, E., Adelman, M., & Gregory, C. (2009). Intersections of immigration and domestic violence: Voices of battered immigrant women. *Feminist Criminology*, *4*(32), 32–56.

Erez, E., & Harper, S. (2018). Intersectionality, immigration, and domestic violence. In R. Martínez, M. E. Hollis, & J. I. Stowell. *The handbook of race, ethnicity, crime, and justice.* Hoboken, NJ: John Wiley & Sons, Inc. (pp. 457–474).

Ford, M., Acosta, A., & Sutcliffe, T. J. (2013). Beyond terminology: The policy impact of a grassroots movement. *Intellectual and Developmental Disabilities*, *51*(2), 108–112.

Friedman, C. (2016). Outdated language: Use of "mental retardation" in Medicaid HCBS waivers post-Rosa's Law. *Intellectual and Developmental Disabilities*, *54*(4), 342–353.

Goffman, E. (1963). *Stigma: Notes on the management of spoiled identity*. New York, NY: Simon & Shuster, Inc.

Hewitt, J. P., & Shulman, D. (2011). *Self and society: A symbolic interactionist social psychology*, 11th edition. Boston, MA: Allyn & Bacon.

Koegler, E., Howland, W., Gibbons, P., Teti, M., & Hanni, S. (2020). "When her visa expired, the family refused to renew it," intersections of human trafficking and domestic violence: Qualitative document analysis of case examples from a major Midwest City. *Journal of Interpersonal Violence*. [Advance online publication]. doi: 10.1177/0886260520957978

Leisenring, A. (2006). Confronting "victim" discourses: The identity work of battered women. *Symbolic Interaction*, *29*(3), 307–330.

Murray, C. E., & Crowe, A. (2017). *Overcoming the stigma of intimate partner abuse*. New York and London: Routledge.

Olivas, M. A. (2020). *Perchance to DREAM: A legal and political history of the DREAM act & DACA*. New York, NY: New York University Press.

Orloff, L. E., & Kaguyutan, J. V. (2002). Offering a helping hand: Legal protections for battered immigrant women: A history of legislative responses. *Gender, Social Policy, & the Law*, *10*(1), 95–170.

Polaris Project. (n.d.). *2019 data report: The U.S. National Human Trafficking Hotline*. Retrieved from https://polarisproject.org/wp-content/uploads/2019/09/Polaris-2019-US-National-Human-Trafficking-Hotline-Data-Report.pdf

Reynolds, B. (2021). Reforming and clarifying special immigrant juvenile status. *Journal of Legislation*, *47*(1), 112–132.

4 Extending Surveillance and Social Control

This chapter analyzes IMR-related IPV statutes through the lens of surveillance and social control. Its contents first summarize the intersectional implications of surveillance and social control. Then, the chapter looks at the complexities of social control, including the operationalization of social control within statutes. The chapter reports on the percentage of statutes that were coded as extending social control into the lives of IMR IPV victim-survivors. Discussions and implications are provided accordingly.

Intersectionality, Surveillance, and Social Control

Although the apex of punishment—public torture—was not levied as frequently in later times when compared to the eighteenth century, punishment itself shed its pre-existing form, continuing with lesser severity but no less intent on control (Foucault, 1995). This means of transformation from one punishment mechanism to another, in a general sense, can be likened to the idea that racism, classism, and sexism tend to also shed pre-existing forms, continuing "underground" as less pronounced but no less intent on domination (see Massey, 2007). Racism, sexism, and classism make their interwoven existences known in the lives of Black women, other women of color, and poor women through mechanisms that in turn reproduce and perpetuate such systems of inequality. In this context, such mechanisms, like the carceral and child welfare systems, inject surveillance and social control into the lives of marginalized women (Crenshaw, 2013). Accordingly, the racism-sexism-classism intersection morphs and permutates across time in ever-changing ways—including through means of surveillance and social control (see Appendix Figure A.2).

DOI: 10.4324/9781003167044-4

Across-Time Permutation of Inequality

While the formal dismantling of discrimination for groups like women (voting rights) and African Americans (the end of slavery) occurred historically, the broader foundations that prop up oppressive structures generally shed their pre-existing forms (Massey, 2007). When dismantled, an oppressive mechanism's residue finds loopholes in the attitudinal and legal contracts of society so it can still be relevant across time as society becomes less tolerant of the pre-existing level of inequality. For example, in the U.S., slavery shifted into Jim Crow laws—which further morphed into hyper-incarceration that plagued (and still plagues) the Black community. Undercutting of social programs, barriers to legal entry, and increased interior immigration enforcement targeted persons who "look" and "sound" a certain way, profoundly affecting the Latinx community (Massey, 2007).

Like race, gender and class stratification have also morphed over time. At the axis of class, the mid-1900's changed labor laws shifted over time to cuts in social spending (e.g., welfare) and disproportionate tax burden on persons of middle and lower socioeconomic status. The foundational segmenting of white-collar jobs into pink-collar instilled gender segregation into the professional realm. Stratification then shifted toward women's increased engagement in family labor (Massey, 2007). The gendered occupational structure morphed into being stratified by class (Massey, 2007) and burdened women with a "second shift" (i.e., unpaid housework atop working for pay outside the household; Hochschild & Machung, 2012; see also, Disch, 2006). In sum, inequality does not go away but transforms into something new and more stubborn to mitigate.

Intersectionality

Historically, movements aiming to improve the status of certain groups have been singular in their approaches. That is, they aim to advance the rights of one group in reaction to one system of oppression (Crenshaw, 1989, 1991; Roschelle, 2017). The problem with this approach is that its analysis brings inadequate force to take on, not just one system of oppression but a series of oppressive systems (Collins & Bilge, 2020). For example, the civil rights movement took on racism. The feminist movement took on sexism. However, in this process of taking on separate oppressive systems, the needs of Black women were ignored (Crenshaw, 1989). The prescription for this ignoring of intersections is the need to analyze and mobilize against various systems of oppression simultaneously (Crenshaw, 1989; Collins & Bilge, 2020).[1]

Surveillance and Social Control

Surveillance and social control are manifestations of intersecting oppressive systems that are felt in lived experience. Crenshaw (2013) reviewed three studies, which show how intersecting inequalities create surveillance and social control through:

- public housing and the policing system, in which Black women receiving Section 8 in mostly white communities were monitored and had their houses searched;
- child welfare and the mass incarceration system, in which those deemed already to deserve punishment are given punishment, which reinforces the function of the intersecting systems; and
- child welfare and the immigration system, in which immigrant women must project the idea of a good mother when facing the immigration system.

In these ways, different versions of hardships within lived experience permutate from intersection to intersection.

Complexities of Surveillance and Social Control

The complexities of surveillance and social control for IPV victim-survivors, violence-perpetrating partners, the State,[2] and marginalized communities are complex:

> Given the complex relationship of women of color, indigenous women, poor women, queer folks, immigrants, sex workers and other women vulnerable to being criminalized by the justice system, the assumption that surveillance measures can provide protection to VAW victims is problematic. In particular, surveillance technologies that deepen existing links to the prison industrial complex pose problems for victims and anti-violence advocates.
>
> (Mason & Magnet, 2012, p. 114)

For example, the State levies surveillance against immigrants in several ways, such as through the threat (and actual action) of raids, detention, and removal/deportation (for discussions of these topics, see Menjívar, Cervantes, & Alvord, 2017). Further, immigrant enforcement has a decentralized tendency. A multifaceted way in which the State wields the power of immigration enforcement deals with the collaboration between the federal government and local jurisdictions (see Armenta & Alvarez, 2017). According to Graber and Avila (2019), in the 2018–2019 time period, "83 [counties in the U.S.] had some form of affirmative agreement to conduct immigration enforcement under the 287(g) program, and 190 had contracts to rent bed space to ICE for immigration detention" (p. 9).

Violence-perpetrating partners employ tactics that mimic surveillance through control and stalking behaviors, specifically monitoring. For example, 25.5 percent of women and 24.9 percent of men in the 2015 NISVS reported that their partners "kept track" of them by "demanding" to know their location and activities (Smith et al., 2018). Dardis, Ahrens, Howard, and Mechanic (2020) examined intimate partner surveillance (IPS) in the context of intimate partner abuse (IPA), finding that IPS was common in such contexts and was present in the experiences of over half of women who experienced IPA. Some of these tactics were qualitatively described as physical monitoring (e.g., following), electronic monitoring (e.g., checking internet browsing history), and having the survivor report back to the violence-perpetrating partner (e.g., checking in). Through a person-centered analysis, Dardis et al. (2020) identified two patterns of violence. One pattern featured the presence of lower levels of IPA in the absence of surveillance tactics. The other pattern featured the presence of higher levels of IPA totally dominated by surveillance tactics.

Shifting to looking at structures, government policies can result in programs that regulate the lives of marginalized IPV survivors. For example, welfare work requirements may regulate the experiences of women who experience poverty through work participation requirements, child support enforcement cooperation pressure, and various "sanction mechanisms" (see Josephson, 2005). This formal social control (by the State) can intersect with informal social control (e.g., domestic violence; Josephson, 2002). Other forms of State control, such as victim arrest and the threat of deportation, may increase the risk of further violence (see Coker, 2005). In this context, surveillance can be operationalized through the idea of *social control*. Josephson (2005) puts forth that social control represents "the imposition of specific behavioral requirements that must be met by recipients of public benefits in order to maintain their eligibility for those benefits" (p. 88). The application of surveillance through social control to IMR-related IPV state-level policies offers the opportunity for an understanding of the role of the State in regulating parts of victim-survivors' lives.

Statutes, Surveillance, and Social Control

About 33 percent (*n* = 24) of statutes concerning IMR victim-survivors of IPV featured, in some way, the imposition of requirements in exchange for benefit and protection eligibility. For example, Section 679.10 of the California Penal Code makes helpfulness in prosecuting perpetrators as a requirement for protection:

> Upon the request of the victim, victim's family member, licensed attorney representing the victim, or representative fully accredited by the United States Department of Justice authorized to represent the victim in immigration proceedings, a certifying official from a certifying entity shall certify victim helpfulness on the Form I-918 Supplement B certification, when the victim was a victim of a qualifying criminal activity and has been helpful, is being helpful, or is likely to be helpful to the detection or investigation or prosecution of that qualifying criminal activity.
>
> (Cal. Pen. Code § 679.10)

In this context, the head of entities such as law enforcement agencies can confirm whether a victim is helpful regarding the U-visa petition form. While this provision may be helpful to victim-survivors, it must be remembered that it was adopted in the context of larger surveillance and social control system. The requirement of "helpfulness," in this context, is determined by the state. This determination by the state is a factor in the determination of protection by the state. IMR IPV victim-survivors may be tied to the state in all aspects of the process. On one end, protection from deportation and detention can offer victim-survivors enhanced "power in relation to their partners or former partners," at the same time, being "helpful" as a key requirement in helping the state meet carceral ends could "disempower" victim-survivors (Josephson, 2005, p. 97).

In another example, Section 908.104 of the Florida Statutes puts forth provisions that align law enforcement agency efforts with those of federal immigration enforcement—such as honoring immigration detainers. However, government entities do not have to provide federal immigration entities with information on crime victims/witnesses. However, this is contingent upon if the victim/witness "timely and in good faith responds to the entity's or agency's request for information and cooperation in the investigation or prosecution of the offense" (Fla. Stat. § 908.104). Similarly to Section 679.10 of the California Penal Code, Florida Statutes Section 908.104 requires a tradeoff—trading "good faith," timeliness, and cooperation for protection from federal immigration enforcement. In this case, there is an "imposition of specific behavioral requirements that must be met" for survivors to receive protection (Josephson, 2005, p. 97).

One statute mentions deeming and citizenship requirements, specifically regarding medical assistance. Section 256B.06 of the Minnesota Statutes states as follows:

> (a) Eligibility for medical assistance is limited to citizens of the United States, qualified noncitizens as defined in this subdivision, and other persons residing lawfully in the United States.... (b) "Qualified noncitizen" means a person who meets one of the following immigration criteria: ... (7) determined to be a battered noncitizen by the United States Attorney General according to the Illegal Immigration Reform and Immigrant Responsibility Act of 1996, title V of the Omnibus Consolidated Appropriations Bill, Public Law 104-200; ... Subd. 5. Deeming of sponsor income and resources. When determining eligibility for any federal or state funded medical assistance under this section, the income and resources of all noncitizens shall be deemed to include their sponsors' income and resources as required under the Personal Responsibility and Work Opportunity Reconciliation Act of 1996, title IV, Public Law 104-193, sections 421 and 422, and subsequently set out in federal rules.
>
> (Minn. Stat. § 256B.06)

Here, eligibility determination rests on the reconsideration of income/resources.

Another example of the imposition of requirement, while broader, is Section 13283 of the California Welfare and Institutions Code:

> Notwithstanding any other provision of law, the department shall ensure that noncitizen victims of trafficking, domestic violence, and other serious crimes ... have access to refugee cash assistance, and refugee employment social services set forth in this chapter, to the same extent as individuals who are admitted to the United States as refugees under Section 1157 of Title 8 of the United States Code. These individuals shall be subject to the same work requirements and exemptions as other participants, provided that compliance with these requirements is authorized by law.
>
> (Cal. Wel. & Inst. Code § 13283)

Work requirements may be very difficult to attain or "nearly impossible" in the context of IPV (Josephson, 2005, p. 95). IMR IPV victim-survivors with certain statuses, such as undocumented status, may face compounded difficulties.

Discussion

The present analysis exposes the theme of decentralization in surveillance within policy. Indeed, surveillance may be scattered throughout society (e.g., spilling over from prisons to schools, hospitals, etc.) increasingly across time to the point in which compliance at the individual level is automatic (see Foucault, 1995). As shown in Chapter 3, there is generally a lag between the adoption and enactment of federal policy and the adoption and enactment of subnational policies (see Appendix Figure A.3). Federal policies can be viewed as centralized outputs. Subnational policies are decentralized outputs. As the number of IMR IPV statutes have cumulatively increased over time, the cumulative number of surveillance/social control IMR IPV policies has also increased, hinting at a potential decentralization and scattering of surveillance and social control within the policy realm.

While state-level policies targeting IMR status and IPV may be helpful to some extent for victim-survivors, a critical eye must be applied to the surveillance and social control that accompanies such avenues of assistance. Indeed, social control predominantly being levied through federal means (e.g., needing to be helpful for U-visas, needing to be of good character for self-petition) has shifted to many states. In these contexts, the transactional nature of the policy itself means that IMR victim-survivors of IPV may need to meet behavioral requirements for a federal program, specifically to receive further assistance from a state-level program.

One question that arises from this analysis is whether laws leave IMR victim-survivors open to surveillance by more insidious forces. Section 908.104 of the Florida Statutes shows that insidiousness can lie just below the surface of helpfulness. This particular statute institutes the requirement for local law enforcement to assist with federal immigration enforcement. However, it also states that the powers wielded by federal-local collaboration, such as the detainer, would not be directed toward victims of crime, including domestic violence. Yet, the extent to which this provision is helpful may be limited. In essence, it can be interpreted that the State is saying "We have this very scary thing we could do to you, but we *might* not use it against you."

The racism-classism-sexism intersection permutates across time to exact harm on marginalized women in ever-changing ways. Indeed, for IMR victim-survivors of IPV, being pinned between abuse and the State is just one manifestation (see Chapter 7). With every new policy measure intended to help these victim-survivors, a new problem becomes prominent. For example, when the Battered Spouse Waiver came into existence, "immigrant women, particularly immigrant women of color," did not have access to documentation that unlocked its protection because of decreased access to resources that would provide such documentation (Crenshaw, 1991). As another example, the U-visa engages in panoptics and economics of pain, in which the State digs deeply into the life stories of IMR IPV survivors to excavate their pain and suffering, then uses such pain and suffering as currency in a transaction for protection (Abbasi, 2020). From the current research, the most recent permutations involve (a) the decentralization of such commodification, (b) the splicing of IMR IPV with public benefits surveillance, and (c) the state's wielding local-federal immigration enforcement in the face of "offering protection" for victim-survivors.

Conclusion

This chapter looked at surveillance, as measured through social control, within state-level statutes targeting IPV in IMR lives. Over 30 percent of statutes employed language that could be coded as social control, specifically, that requirements exist which must be met to receive or maintain benefits or protection (see Josephson, 2005). The present research found that social control is decentralizing, synthesizing immigration and public benefits policies, and threatening State force while at the same time purporting to protect victim-survivors.

Notes

1. For a more thorough explanation of intersectionality, please see Chapter 6.
2. In this chapter (and others), the term state has two meanings when used as a noun. First, the term can mean one of the 50 major subnational governments within the U.S.; when used in this context, the term is in the lowercase font (e.g., "a state"). Second, the term can be used as a more abstract concept indicating governmental power; when used in this context, the "S" in the term is capitalized (e.g., "the State").

References

Abbasi, G. (2020). Discipline and commoditize: How u-visas exploit the pain of gender-based violence. *Feminist Criminology*, *15*(4), 646–491.

Armenta, A., & Alvarez, I. (2017). Policing immigrants or policing immigration? Understanding local law enforcement participation in immigration control. *Sociological Compass*, *11*(2). doi: 10.1111/soc4.12453

Graber, L., & Avila, K. (2019, December 17). *Growing the resistance: How sanctuary laws and policies have flourished during the Trump administration*. The Immigrant Legal Resource Center. Retrieved from https://www.ilrc.org/sites/default/files/resources/2019.12_sanctuary_report-final-12.17.pdf

Coker, D. (2005). Shifting power for battered women: Law, material resources, and poor women of color. In N. J. Sokoloff, & C. Pratt (Eds.), *Domestic violence at the margins: Readings on race, class, gender, and culture*. New Brunswick, NJ: Rutgers University Press.

Collins, P. H., & Bilge, S. (2020). *Intersectionality.* Medford, MA: Polity Press.

Crenshaw, K. (1989). Demarginalizing the intersection of race and sex: A Black feminist critique of antidiscrimination doctrine, feminist theory and antiracist politics. *University of Chicago Legal Forum*, 139–167.

Crenshaw, K. (1991). Mapping the margins: Intersectionality, identity politics, and violence against women. *Stanford Law Review*, *43*(6), 1241–1299.

Crenshaw, K. W. (2013). From private violence to mass incarceration: Thinking intersectionally about women, race, and social control. *Journal of Scholarly Perspectives*, *9*(01), 23–50. Retrieved from https://escholarship.org/uc/item/7mp3k6m3

Dardis, C. M., Ahrens, C., Howard, R. L., & Mechanic, M. B. (2020). Patterns of surveillance, control, and abuse among a diverse sample of intimate partner abuse survivors. *Violence Against Women* [Advance online publication]. doi: 10.1177/1077801220975497.

Disch, E. (2006). *Reconstructing gender: A multicultural anthology*, 4th edition. New York, NY: The McGraw-Hill Companies, Inc.

Foucault, M. (1995). *Discipline and punish: The birth of the prison*. New York, NY: Vintage Books, A Division of Random House, Inc.

Hochschild, A., & Machung, A. (2012). *The second shift: Working families and the revolution at home*. New York, NY: Penguin Books.

Josephson, J. (2005). The intersectionality of domestic violence and welfare in the lives of poor women. In N. J. Sokoloff, & C. Pratt (Eds.), *Domestic violence at the margins: Readings on race, class, gender, and culture*. New Brunswick, NJ: Rutgers University Press.

Menjívar, C., Cervantes, A. G., & Alvord, D. (2017). The expansion of "crimmigration," mass detention, and deportation. *Sociology Compass*, *12*, 1–15. doi: 10.1111/soc4.12573

Mason, C., & Magnet, S. (2012). Surveillance studies and violence against women. *Surveillance & Society*, *10*(2). Retrieved from https://www.surveillance-and-society.org

Massey, D. S. (2007). *Categorically unequal: The American stratification system.* Russel Sage Foundation.

Roschelle, A. R. (2017, December). Our lives matter: The racialized violence of poverty among homeless mothers of color. *Sociological Forum, 32,* 998–1017.

Smith, S. G., Zhang, X., Basile, K. C., Merrick, M. T., Wang, J., Kresnow, M., & Chen, J. (2018). *The national intimate partner and sexual violence survey (NISVS): 2015 data brief.* Atlanta, GA: National Center for Injury Prevention and Control, Centers for Disease Control and Prevention.

5 Constructing Resource Provision

This chapter draws conceptual inspiration from Smith's (2005) method of inquiry, institutional ethnography, to inform its understanding of how state-level IMR-related IPV statutes position resource development and access. It focuses on how statutes create resources, exempt people from resource restrictions, block access to resources and protection, and expand or streamline access to resources and protection. It also looks for other means of how access to resources and protection is shaped in the context of such statutes.

Standpoint, Collectivization, Ruling Relations, and Public Policy

People's experiences and position in society are the beginning points that paint how they know and see the social world around them, that is, their standpoint. This standpoint "works from the actualities of people's everyday lives and experience" (Smith, 2005, p. 593) and is the "site of people's direct experiencing of the world" (Smith, 1997, p. 37). For example, historically, sociology had a masculinist orientation whereby information, concepts, and so forth were produced from the way men knew the world, glossing over the knowledge that could originate only from experiences derived from being a woman (Appelrouth & Edles, 2008).

Standpoint provides the local entryway for understanding the ruling relations: "that extraordinary yet ordinary complex of relations that are textually mediated, that connect us across space and time and organize our everyday lives" (Smith, 2005, p. 593). The ruling relations work at the extra-local level; that is, they work at a place broader than individuals' immediate experiences and actualities in such a way that they impact such immediate experiences and actualities (Smith, 2005). For example, gender inequality may work at the extra-local level to

DOI: 10.4324/9781003167044-5

impact how women are forced to navigate the world at the local level (e.g., how they may be relegated to the home).

The ruling relations act similarly across contexts in that, like sociology's masculinist orientation, they gloss over understandings of people's lives that can only be derived from understanding lived experience. More specifically, "The ruling relations 'extract' the coordinative and concerting of people's everyday/everynight activities from relations between persons and subject them to specialized and often technical development as 'organization,' 'communication,' 'information,' 'management,' and the like" (Smith, 1997, p. 43). For example, Pence's (2001) work on the police and court system, in part, states that "battered women's lives are twisted into preformulated categories created not in the lived experience, but in the professional discourse" (p. 203).

Standpoints can collate into something broader. The genesis of the women's movement featured women beginning in their experiences, speaking with each other, and sharing descriptions of their actualities. Around these exchanges, women began exposing their experiences by giving them names in a shared vocabulary: "'oppression,' 'rape,' 'harassment,' 'violence,' and others" (Smith, 2005, p. 591). In this way, what women knew and how they saw the world collectivized into the foundation of a political force. It became a movement.

Collations of standpoints can be injected into the political realm and inform policy. For example, some tangible aspects of the Women's Movement's forward progression included the 19th Amendment, which codified women's right to vote. In this way, collations of standpoints changed the ruling relations so that women could further participate in the political realm and affect change regarding their collective status. In this way, a standpoint (e.g., one woman's experience) can join forces with another standpoint (e.g., another woman's experience) to permeate the text (e.g., the Constitution) and rearrange the ruling relations (e.g., mitigating gender inequality). Then, the changes in the ruling relations (e.g., mitigated gender inequality) trickle back through the text (e.g., the 19th Amendment) to bring a new experience at the local level (e.g., the right to vote), which women can then use to etch their standpoints into other texts (e.g., state-level laws) to further change the ruling relations.

Constructing Resources and Protection

The present research starts with a theme from victim-survivor voices in the extant literature: access to resources and protection. Indeed, for IMR victim-survivors of IPV, many forces and phenomena can affect access to resources and protection, from the victim-survivors' reaching out, to whether other persons can or want to provide such assistance. These forces and phenomena can include racism (Silva-Martínez, 2016; Sabri et al., 2018), fear of the legal system's taking away their children (Erez, Adelman, & Gregory, 2009; Kelly, 2009; Salcido & Adelman, 2004; Silva-Martínez, 2016; Vidales, 2010), and language (barriers) (Latta & Goodman, 2005; Reina, Lohman, & Maldonado, 2014; Bhuyan et al., 2005; Silva-Martínez, 2016; Vidales, 2010). Indeed, contexts and forces, like racism and language (barriers), can shape the walls of the maze through which IMR victim-survivors of IPV must navigate to obtain resources, protection, and freedom. To understand how state-level statutes position people in relation to resources, the present research codes for four categories: (a) whether statutes create resources; (b) whether statutes exempt people from resource restrictions; (c) whether statutes block access to resources or protection; and (d) whether statutes expand or streamline access to resources or protection.

Creating, Exempting, Blocking, Expanding, and Streamlining

Creating Resources

About 18 percent ($n = 13$) of statutes were coded as creating resources (see Figure 5.1). These statutes included subjects like grant funding for trauma recovery centers, grant funding for LGBT organizations that target domestic violence, and training for District Attorneys and Assistant District Attorneys. Statutes activated their respective programs and services by using language such as "shall provide," "shall create," "shall develop," and "shall convene." For example, Section 7.98.030 of the Wisconsin Statutes states that "The office of crime victims advocacy shall convene a crime victim certification steering committee" (Wis. Stat. 49.165). In another example, a Massachusetts statute states partly as follows:

> The Massachusetts District Attorneys' Association shall provide training on the issue of domestic violence and sexual violence in the commonwealth, at least once biannually, to all district attorneys and assistant district attorneys. Such training shall include, but not be limited to, the dissemination of information concerning:
>
> 1 misdemeanor and felony offenses in which domestic violence and sexual violence are often involved;

2   the civil rights and remedies available to victims of domestic violence and sexual violence;
3   methods for assessing the degree of risk of homicide involved in situations of domestic violence including, but not limited to, gathering information from the victim regarding the suspect's past reported and non-reported behavior and dangerousness, such as: (i) whether the suspect has ever used a weapon against the victim or threatened the victim with a weapon; (ii) whether the suspect owns a gun; (iii) whether the suspect's physical violence against the victim has increased in severity or frequency; (iv) whether the suspect has threatened to kill the victim; (v) whether the suspect has ever threatened or attempted suicide; (vi) whether the suspect has used or threatened physical violence against the victim's family, other household members or pets; (vii) whether the suspect uses illegal drugs; (viii) whether the suspect abuses alcohol; and (ix) whether there have been specific instances of strangulation or suffocation of the victim by the suspect;
4   law enforcement techniques, information sharing and methods of promoting cooperation among different areas of law enforcement in combating domestic violence and sexual violence, including the importance of keeping victims informed as to the whereabouts of suspected abusers and other such information helpful for victim safety planning;
5   the physiological and psychological effects of the pattern of domestic violence and sexual violence on its victims, including children who witness such abuse;
6   the increased vulnerability of victims who are gay, lesbian, bisexual, transgender, low-income, minority or immigrant, and including training on ways in which the indicators of dangerousness in these communities may be different from those in non-marginalized communities ... (ALM GL ch. 12, § 33)

Exemptions from Resource Restrictions

Thirty-six percent (n = 26) of statutes, in some way, exempted people from resource restrictions. Concerning public benefits was a common occurrence among the resource exemption statutes. In these contexts, words like "exempt" and "except" were utilized to some degree. Other statutes used phrases like "shall not apply" or "shall be waived." In these statutes, a restriction on eligibility may be placed on certain groups, with certain sub-groups being exempt from ineligibility

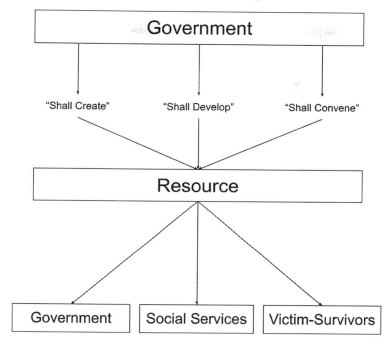

Figure 5.1 Depiction of resource flows within state-level statutes.

standards. For example, Section 31-13-7 of the Alabama Code puts forth such standards:

a As used in this section, the following terms have the following meanings:

  1 EMERGENCY MEDICAL CONDITION. The same meaning as provided in 42 U.S.C. § 1396b(v)(3).
  2 FEDERAL PUBLIC BENEFITS. The same meaning as provided in 8 U.S.C. § 1611.
  3 STATE OR LOCAL PUBLIC BENEFITS. The same meaning as provided in 8 U.S.C. § 1621.

b An alien who is not lawfully present in the United States and who is not defined as an alien eligible for public benefits under 8 U.S.C. § 1621(a) or 8 U.S.C. § 1641 shall not receive any state or local public benefits.

c Except as otherwise provided in subsection (e) or where exempted by federal law, commencing on September 1, 2011, each agency or political subdivision of the state shall verify with the federal government the lawful presence in the United States of each alien who applies for state or local public benefits, pursuant to 8 U.S.C. §§ 1373(c), 1621, and 1625.

d   An agency of this state or a county, city, town, or other political subdivision of this state may not consider race, color, or national origin in the enforcement of this section.

e   Verification of lawful presence in the United States shall not be required for any of the following:

1   For primary or secondary school education, and state or local public benefits that are listed in 8 U.S.C. § 1621(b).

2   For obtaining health care items and services that are necessary for the treatment of an emergency medical condition of the person involved and are not related to an organ transplant procedure.

3   For short term, noncash, in kind emergency disaster relief.

4   For public health assistance for immunizations with respect to immunizable diseases, for the Special Supplemental Nutrition Program for Women, Infants, and Children, and for testing and treatment of symptoms of communicable diseases, whether or not such symptoms are caused by a communicable disease.

5   For programs, services, or assistance, such as soup kitchens, crisis counseling and intervention, and short-term shelter specified by federal law or regulation that satisfy all of the following:

a   Deliver in-kind services at the community level, including services through public or private nonprofit agencies.

b   Do not condition the provision of assistance, the amount of assistance provided, or the cost of assistance provided on the income or resources of the individual recipient.

c   Are necessary for the protection of life or safety.

6   For prenatal care.

7   For child protective services and adult protective services and domestic violence services workers. (Ala. Code § 31-13-7)

Here, the actions that would need to take place (i.e., lawful presence verification) on the part of social service providers (e.g., domestic violence services workers) "shall not be required," which may partly shield certain IMR victim-survivors of IPV from the potential wrath of the State.

Blocking, Expanding, and Streamlining
Access to Resources or Protection

Four statutes were coded as blocking access to resources or protection for *some* group of people. All of these statutes targeted public benefits. For example, in relation to Minnesota's Family investment Program, "an undocumented immigrant who resides in the United States without the approval or acquiescence of the United States Citizenship and Immigration Services is not eligible for MFIP" (Minn. Stat. § 256J.11). In defining the parameters of (in)eligibility for public social services, Section 18945 of the California Welfare and Institutions Code states that

> After one year from the date of application for public social services, noncitizen victims of a severe form of trafficking, as defined in paragraph (1) of subdivision (b), shall be ineligible for state-funded services if a visa application has not been filed until under Section 1101(a)(15)(T)(i) or (ii) of Title 8 of the United States Code.
>
> (Cal. Wel. & Inst. Code § 18945)

Eight statutes were coded as expanding and/or streamlining access to resources or protection. These statutes ranged from targeting health, public benefits, and criminal justice/law enforcement. The California Government Code focuses its expansion/streamlining of access to resources and protection via health. For example, one statute reads, in part,

> (e)The board, when considering grant applications, shall give preference to a trauma recovery center that conducts outreach to, and serves, both of the following:
> (1)Crime victims who typically are unable to access traditional services, including, but not limited to, victims who are homeless, chronically mentally ill, of diverse ethnicity, members of immigrant and refugee groups, disabled, who have severe trauma-related symptoms or complex psychological issues, or juvenile victims, including minors who have had contact with the juvenile dependency or justice system.
>
> (Cal Gov Code § 13963.1)

Here, there is a streamlining of access for trauma recovery centers that help underserved populations, such as immigrants and refugees.

Discussion

Findings

In coding IMR-related IPV statutes for constructing resource and/or protection access and development, the present research found that:

- 18 percent (*n* = 13) of statutes created resources;
- 36 percent (*n* = 26) of statutes enacted exemptions from resource restrictions;
- 6 percent (*n* = 4) of statutes blocked access to resources or protection; and
- 11 percent (*n* = 8) of statutes expanded or streamlined access to resources or protection.

Resource creation statutes implemented government-oriented, social service-oriented, and victim-survivor-oriented resources. Some provided training for officials (e.g., district attorneys). Others provided services (e.g., cash assistance, medical assistance) to visa applicants. Other statutes provided funding to organizations. Resource shifting statutes redirected resources from one person or entity to others. For example, one statute transferred funds from perpetrators, using the government to transfer funds to organizations, which would then (hopefully) help victim-survivors (Cal Pen Code § 1463.27). Resource/protection access blocking statutes utilized links between words to structure ineligibility. Resource/protection access expansion/streamline statutes utilized a similar strategy, but instead for opening up access (for a more in-depth discussion, see the "Terminological and Definitional Grounds of Resource and Protection Access" section of this chapter).

Connecting Theory and Findings

This chapter drew inspiration from Smith's (1997, 2005) method of inquiry to develop an understanding of how state-level IMR-related IPV statutes construct development and access to resources. In accordance with this approach, standpoints are collectivized, codified in text, and alter ruling relations, which in turn set the boundaries within which people can define themselves, know, and interact with the world around them. Similarly, they can define and set the boundaries through which people navigate the world. For IMR victim-survivors of IPV, state-level statutes, as texts, translate the will of the broader ruling relations into the local parts of their experiences. Indeed, experiences like racism and language barriers shape the maze though which victim-survivors must venture.

Over the years, advocates and other actors have pressed for greater protection of IMR victim-survivors of IPV from abuse and the State. These collectivized standpoints placed pressure on policymakers to change the text of existing law. Some outputs of these efforts include the Battered Spouse Waiver, the Self-Petition, and the U-visa (see Chapters 1 and 3). In changing federal legal texts, the ruling relations were also partially changed in that inequalities were, *to some extent*, mitigated. While other issues presented themselves (e.g., surveillance and social control; see Chapter 4), these changes to the text had an impact on some women's lives through mitigating the wrath of the State.

To look at how viewpoints and perspectives translate into policy, we can look at state-to-state partisan legislative control in relation to the effective dates of statutes that construct resource access.[1] For example, of the resource exemption statutes with a known effective date ($n = 22$),[2] most ($n = 14$) had effective dates that occurred during Democratic state legislative control; seven of these st[...] had effective dates that occurred under Republican co[...], and one under "split"[3] legislative control. Of the resour[...] [...]ation statutes with a known effective date ($n = 11$),[4] most [...] 9) had effective dates that occurred during a Democratic [...] legislative control; two of these statutes had effective da[...] [...]at occurred under Republican legislative control. Of the [...] [...]urce access blocking statutes ($n = 4$), which contained at l[...] [...]ne provision that blocked access to a resource in some wa[...] [...]ost ($n = 3$) were enacted under Democratic legislative cont[...] while one became effective under Republican legislative con-
t[...]. A similar trend can be seen in statutes that streamline access to resources, in which six and two statutes became effective under Democratic and Republican legislative control, respectively. These figures show that, while there is a trend in partisan adoption of these statutes, the details are accompanied by nuance. A specific example of this nuance is embodied in a surprise, specifically Section 402.87 of the Florida Statutes, which sanctions the development of a structure to provide services/benefits to domestic violence and human trafficking survivors. The surprising nature of this development is embodied in its being effective in a southern and Republican-controlled state.

Terminological and Definitional Grounds of Resource and Protection Access

The present research found two overarching means by which access to resources was structured. First, certain language (words) was coordinated in some statutes to restrict or open eligibility. Second, individual words (terms) themselves are defined in such a way that definitions block certain populations from access. Indeed, access may be embedded in the very terms that define status. For example, Florida provides legal definitional parameters for both dating violence (based on a "dating relationship") and domestic violence (based on "family or household" members).[5] Section 908.104 of the Florida Statute exempts "any alien unlawfully present" who is a "witness or victim of a crime of domestic violence" from being subject to information sharing on the part of the State that could be used in immigration detention:

> This section does not apply to any alien unlawfully present in the United States if he or she is or has been a necessary witness or victim of a crime of domestic violence, rape, sexual exploitation, sexual assault, murder, manslaughter, assault, battery, human trafficking, kidnapping, false imprisonment, involuntary servitude, fraud in foreign labor contracting, blackmail, extortion, or witness tampering.

However, given the way that Florida bisects IPV into dating violence and domestic violence, one must ask if "any alien unlawfully present" who is a witness or victim to *dating violence* can also access this protection from the State.

Connecting back to the theoretical and conceptual grounds of this chapter, we see that the experience of venturing through the legal terrain of these statutes changes based on who is navigating it. IMR victim-survivors of IPV are not a singular group. Thinking separately, the acronym IMR includes many statuses and identities, like refugees, lawful permanent residents, naturalized citizens, and others. Likewise, there are different types of IPV based on relationship and the nature of violent acts: psychological violence, dating violence, spousal violence, sexual violence, and others. There are undocumented dating violence victims, permanent resident spousal violence victims, and others. Just as standpoints are the access points to understanding text and ruling relations, the statuses of IMR IPV victim-survivors are the starting point to how they will navigate the text of federal and state law, which is impacted by the ruling relations that such texts mediate.

Conclusion

Overall, statute-to-statute constructs of resource and protection access are diverse. However, in general, statutes state which groups are eligible or ineligible. Wrapped around these statements of (in)eligibility are specific words (e.g., *qualified alien*, *undocumented immigrant*,

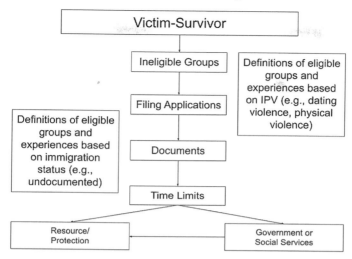

Figure 5.2 Depiction of how terms shape navigation of resources.

domestic violence, battering or extreme cruelty) with underlying definitions that may further define the parameters of eligibility. Eligibility may require the completion of applications and providing of supporting documentation. Time limits may be placed on resource provision based on whether documents/applications are filed. Victim-survivors must then reach into the government or social service realm to reach a particular resource or protection (see Figure 5.2; for additional context, see Chapter 8).

Notes

1. For this analysis, we looked at the partisan composition of state legislatures for respective statutes in respective years (National Conference of State Legislatures, 2013, 2014, 2015, 2016, 2018, n.d.a, n.d.b, n.d.c). With the available data, the partisan composition could not be identified for certain years (i.e., some odd-numbered years). To account for this phenomenon, we imputed the missing partisan composition for a particular year (e.g., 1997) with the previous year (e.g., 1996). This was completed for 10 statutes.
2. Four of the resource exemption statutes had an effective date that could not be identified for the IMR-IPV intersection.
3. "Split" legislative control means that neither party had total control of the state legislature (e.g., a Democratic state house and a Republican state senate).
4. Two of the resource creation statutes had an effective date that could not be identified for the IMR-IPV intersection.

5. According to the Florida statutes,
   "Domestic violence" means any assault, aggravated assault, battery, aggravated battery, sexual assault, sexual battery, stalking, aggravated stalking, kidnapping, false imprisonment, or any criminal offense resulting in physical injury or death of one family or household member by another family or household member. (Fla. Stat. 741.28)
   Additionally,
   "Dating violence" means violence between individuals who have or have had a continuing and significant relationship of a romantic or intimate nature. The existence of such a relationship shall be determined based on the consideration of the following factors:
   1. A dating relationship must have existed within the past 6 months;
   2. The nature of the relationship must have been characterized by the expectation of affection or sexual involvement between the parties; and
   3. The frequency and type of interaction between the persons involved in the relationship must have included that the persons have been involved over time and on a continuous basis during the course of the relationship. (Fla. Stat 784.046)

References

Appelrouth, S., & Edles, L. D. (2008). *Classical and contemporary sociological theory: Text and readings*. Thousand Oaks, CA: Pine Forge Press.

Bhuyan, R., Mell, M., Senturia, K., Sullivan, M., & Shiu-Thornton, S. (2005). "Women must endure according to their karma" Cambodian immigrant women talk about domestic violence. *Journal of Interpersonal Violence*, *20*(8), 902–921.

Erez, E., Adelman, M., & Gregory, C. (2009). Intersections of immigration and domestic violence: Voices of battered immigrant women. *Feminist criminology*, *4*(1), 32–56.

Kelly, U. A. (2009). "I'm a mother first": The influence of mothering in the decision-making processes of battered immigrant Latino women. *Research in Nursing & Health*, *32*(3), 286–297.

Latta, R. E., & Goodman, L. A. (2005). Considering the interplay of cultural context and service provision in intimate partner violence: The case of Haitian immigrant women. *Violence Against Women*, *11*(11), 1441–1464.

National Conference of State Legislatures. (2013, January 31). *2013 State and legislative partisan composition* [PDF file].

National Conference of State Legislatures. (2014, June 9). *2014 State and legislative partisan composition* [PDF file].

National Conference of State Legislatures. (2015, January 25). *2015 State and legislative partisan composition* [PDF file].

National Conference of State Legislatures. (2016, January 29). *2016 State and legislative partisan composition* [PDF file].

National Conference of State Legislatures. (2018, January 10). *2018 State and legislative partisan composition* [PDF file].

National Conference of State Legislatures. (n.d.a). *Partisan composition of state legislatures 1978-1988* [PDF file].

National Conference of State Legislatures. (n.d.b). *Partisan composition of state legislatures 1990-2000* [PDF file].

National Conference of State Legislatures. (n.d.c). *Partisan composition of state Legislatures 2002-2014* [PDF file].

Pence, E. (2001). Safety for battered women in a textually mediated legal system. *Studies in Cultures, Organizations, and Societies, 7*(2), 199–229.

Reina, A. S., Lohman, B. J., & Maldonado, M. M. (2014). "He said they'd deport me" factors influencing domestic violence help-seeking practices among Latina immigrants. *Journal of Interpersonal Violence, 29*(4), 593–615.

Sabri, B., Nnawulezi, N., Njie-Carr, V. P., Messing, J., Ward-Lasher, A., Alvarez, C., & Campbell, J. C. (2018). Multilevel risk and protective factors for intimate partner violence among African, Asian, and Latina immigrant and refugee women: Perceptions of effective safety planning interventions. *Race and Social Problems, 10*(4), 348–365.

Salcido, O., & Adelman, M. (2004). "He has me tied with the blessed and damned papers": Undocumented-immigrant battered women in Phoenix, Arizona. *Human Organization, 63*(2), 162–172.

Silva-Martínez, E. (2016). "El Silencio" conceptualizations of Latina immigrant survivors of intimate partner violence in the Midwest of the United States. *Violence Against Women, 22*(5), 523–544.

Smith, D. (2005). Institutional ethnography. In S. Appelrouth, & L. D. Edles (Eds.), *Classical and contemporary sociological theory: Text and readings* (pp. 591–602). Thousand Oaks, CA: Pine Forge Press.

Smith, D. E. (1997). Consciousness, meaning, and ruling relations: From women's standpoint. In *Millennial milestone: The heritage and future of sociology in the North American region*. Toronto, Canada: Proceedings of the ISA Regional Conference for North America (pp. 37–50).

Vidales, G. T. (2010). Arrested justice: The multifaceted plight of immigrant Latinas who faced domestic violence. *Journal of Family Violence, 25*(6), 533–544.

6 Fostering Inclusion

This chapter draws inspiration from intersectionality to understand if, and to what extent, state-level IMR-related IPV statutes cultivate inclusion, specifically by asking if they mention various demographic backgrounds. Statutes that mention various demographic backgrounds can be roughly grouped into (a) statutes that mention demography in scattered mention, (b) statutes that list demography, and (c) statutes that state intersections.

Intersectionality

Intersectionality disrupts the dichotomous, top-down constructions of identities and oppressive relationships like white/Black, rich/poor, and men/women by exposing intersections (Josephson, 2005). Intersectionality highlights the complexity of human experience as contoured by the simultaneous compounding and nuancing of interacting dimensions of inequality (Collins & Bilge, 2020; Crenshaw, 1989; Josephson, 2005). While the history of this framework cannot be traced in a clean-cut manner, the central ideas of intersectionality were set in motion long ago. Indeed, women of color (e.g., Black women), while still experiencing gendered subjugation, engaged in social justice movements. However, being afforded the media audience for dissemination of ideas was not readily available to Black feminist ideas (Collins & Bilge, 2020).

The Combahee River Collective engaged in/built a social movement-grounded analysis that focused on structures and interconnected means of how systems oppress (Collins & Bilge, 2020). The Combahee River Collective Statement traces the history of Black feminism to "the historical reality of Afro-American women's continuous life-and-death struggle for survival and liberation" (BlackPast, 2012). The statement shows that in the fight for survival and liberation, Black

DOI: 10.4324/9781003167044-6

women activists, both known and unknown, have always existed. In tracing the development of this activism, The Combahee River Collective Statement states that "A combined anti-racist and anti-sexist position drew us together initially, and as we developed politically we addressed ourselves to heterosexism and economic oppression under capitalism" (BlackPast, 2012). In the 1970s and early 1980s, Chicana and African American feminism set the groundwork for intersectionality. In this context, a "shared vocabulary" acknowledging multiplicity in lived experiences was cultivated (Collins & Bilge, 2020).

An intersectional approach to anti-discrimination policy levies a critique of movements that do not center the concerns of human beings who are pushed furthest toward the margins. Instead, singular anti-discrimination forces allow oppressive forces to distract them, thus rendering them restricted to only attempting to enhance rights for a portion of the groups they aim to help, and ultimately helping nobody; that is, mitigating the influence of one system in an individual's or community's experience still exposes them to attacks from the other systems. Bringing Black women's experiences to the center has laid bare the feminist and civil rights movements' historical tendency to gloss over the people at their intersection as time has progressed. Indeed, the prescription to alleviate such erasure has embodied a simultaneous need for anti-racism to integrate feminist thinking, as well as for feminism to integrate anti-racist thinking (Crenshaw, 1989). For example, at the intersection of racism, classism, and sexism, interventions that narrowly target the sexist axis of domination will leave behind women who are at the bottom of the social hierarchy based on race and class (Crenshaw, 1991).

Moreover, an intersectional approach shows that the binding of the anti-violence movement to a criminal legal system that engages in social control was shaped by hardline approaches to issues such as poverty and drugs (Coker & Macquoid, 2015; Crenshaw, 2013), leaving women of color behind in the process of pursuing justice (Crenshaw, 2013). Indeed, in its morphing from grassroots to the mainstream, the anti-violence movement had needed to make it a formidable force in addressing violence against women. The "prison nation" offered to fulfill these needs, thus melding the anti-violence movement to a system of social control (Richie, 2015). Accordingly, there are limits to the helpfulness of interventions targeting social problems when race and class are not considered. Crenshaw (1991) discusses what the present research calls the Battered Spouse Waiver (see Chapter 3). The Battered Spouse Waiver may be out of reach due to limited access to resources that unlock documentation for claiming the waiver for immigrant women of various backgrounds inherent to their lived experiences like cultural identity and class (e.g., because of language barriers, informal norms of living in intergenerational households; Crenshaw, 1991)

In these contexts, "critical race and feminist legal scholars have identified as western law's fundamental problem: the inability to see and hear intersectionally" (McKinnon, 2016, "Introduction," para. 7). The present research dedicates a category of its content analysis to measuring the mention of various groups, specifically to see if any laws engage in a very basic practice: acknowledging intersections of identities and/or statuses. In the coding scheme, the researchers asked whether individual statutes mention various demographic backgrounds. While basic in operationalization, the category—a "yes"/"no" response scheme—is used to determine if and how statutes cultivate inclusion.

How Statutes Frame Status and Identity

About twenty-six percent of statutes ($n = 19$) were categorized as mentioning various demographic backgrounds. These statutes targeted topics like status verification for public benefits, grant funding for trauma recovery centers, restitution that funds domestic violence programs, access to nursing home care and community-based services, international child abduction considerations and risk factors, and other topics. Qualitatively, these statutes can be summarized as belonging to three sub-categories: scattered mentions of statuses, listing statuses, and acknowledging intersections (see Table 6.1).

Table 6.1 Mentions of Various Backgrounds within Statutes ($n = 19$)

Category	n	%
Mentions demographic backgrounds in a scattered manner. That is, they mention more than two backgrounds, but such backgrounds are mentioned at different areas of the statute.	9	47.37 (12.50)
Mentions demographic backgrounds in the form of a list.	15	78.94 (20.83)
Mentions demographic backgrounds in the form of intersections. That is, they pair different statuses with each other.	2	10.53 (2.78)

Note: Number and percentage out of the total number ($N = 72$) of statutes in parentheses.

Scattered Status Mentions

Approximately thirteen percent of total statutes featured scattered mentions of demographic statuses. That is, they mentioned more than two backgrounds, but such backgrounds were mentioned at different areas of the statute (see Panel B of Appendix Figure A.4). These statutes mentioned backgrounds like illegal aliens, incarcerated persons, supplemental security income recipients, age, veterans, and persons near the poverty level. For example, Section 17b-342 of the Connecticut General Statutes mentioned immigration status, persons near the poverty level, and veteran status:

(a) The Commissioner of Social Services shall administer the Connecticut home-care program for the elderly state-wide in order to prevent the institutionalization of elderly persons (1) who are recipients of medical assistance, (2) who are eligible for such assistance, (3) who would be eligible for medical assistance if residing in a nursing facility, or (4) who meet the criteria for the state-funded portion of the program under subsection (i) of this section... Only a United States citizen or a noncitizen who meets the citizenship requirements for eligibility under the Medicaid program shall be eligible for home-care services under this section, except a qualified alien, as defined in Section 431 of Public Law 104-193, admitted into the United States on or after August 22, 1996, or other lawfully residing immigrant alien determined eligible for services under this section prior to July 1, 1997, shall remain eligible for such services... (2) Except for persons residing in affordable housing under the assisted living demonstration project established pursuant to section 17b-347e, as provided in subdivision (3) of this subsection, any person whose income is at or below two hundred per cent of the federal poverty level and who is ineligible for Medicaid shall contribute seven per cent of the cost of his or her care. Any person whose income exceeds two hundred per cent of the federal poverty level shall contribute seven per cent of the cost of his or her care in addition to the amount of applied income determined in accordance with the methodology established by the Department of Social Services for recipients of medical assistance... (l) In determining eligibility for the program described in this section, the commissioner shall not consider as income Aid and Attendance pension benefits granted to a veteran, as defined in section 27-103, or the surviving spouse of such veteran.

(Conn. Gen. Stat. § 17b-342)

Listing Statuses

Approximately twenty-one percent of total statutes simply listed statuses (see Panel A of Appendix Figure A.4). For example, Section 5-2-1-9 of the Indiana Annotated Code, in discussing cultural diversity awareness, discussed "race, religion, gender, age, domestic violence, national origin, and physical and mental disabilities," as well as "persons with autism, mental illness, intellectual disabilities, and developmental disabilities" (Ind. Code Ann. 5-2-1-9). Other statutes mentioned, for example, statuses like "gay, lesbian, bisexual, low-income, minority, immigrant or non-English speaking" (ALM GL ch. 12, § 264).

Some statutes discussed statuses in terms of anti-discrimination (Al. Code § 31-13-7; Fla. Stat. § 414.095; S.C. Code Ann. § 8-29-10). In discussing eligibility for services and temporary cash assistance, Section 414.095 of the Florida Statutes states as follows:

1   (9) OPPORTUNITIES AND OBLIGATIONS.—An applicant for temporary cash assistance has the following opportunities and obligations:

    a   To participate in establishing eligibility by providing facts with respect to circumstances that affect eligibility and by obtaining, or authorizing the department to obtain, documents or information from others in order to establish eligibility.

    b   To have eligibility determined without discrimination based on race, color, sex, age, marital status, handicap, religion, national origin, or political beliefs. (Fla. Stat. § 414.095)

Section 8-29-10 of the South Carolina Annotated Code, in setting forth the legal parameters of presence in the U.S. states the provisions of the statute will be carried out "regard to race, religion, gender, ethnicity, or national origin" (S.C. Code Ann. § 8-29-10).

Acknowledging Intersections

It seems that two statutes, at least clearly, acknowledged intersections. These statutes paired different statuses with each other (see Panel C of Appendix Figure A.4). One statute that acknowledges intersections is Section 13823.17 of the California Penal Code, which reads in part as follows:

    (a) (b) The goal of this section is to establish a targeted or directed grant program for the development and support of domestic violence programs and services for the gay, lesbian, bisexual, and transgender community. The Office of Emergency Services shall use funds from the Equality in Prevention and Services for Domestic Abuse Fund to award grants annually to qualifying organizations, with at least one in southern California and one in northern California, to fund domestic violence programs and services that are specific to the lesbian, gay, bisexual, and transgender community, including, but not limited to, any of the following:...2) The following criteria shall be used to evaluate grant proposals:

a   Whether the proposed program or services would further the purpose of promoting healthy, nonviolent relationships in the lesbian, gay, bisexual, and transgender community.

b   Whether the proposed program or services would reach a significant number of people in, and have the support of, the lesbian, gay, bisexual, and transgender community.

c   Whether the proposed program or services are grounded in a firm understanding of lesbian, gay, bisexual, and transgender domestic violence and represent an innovative approach to addressing the issue.

d   Whether the proposed program or services would reach unique and underserved sectors of the lesbian, gay, bisexual, and transgender community, such as youth, people of color, immigrants, and transgender persons... (Cal Pen Code § 13823.17)

In this statute, the grant evaluation criteria include whether the program/services target—for example—LGBT youth, LGBT people of color, and LGBT immigrants.

The other instance of statutes acknowledging intersections includes a New York law. In discussing the regulation of violence prevention and intervention, requires the following:

... participation of all employees of a child protective service in a training course which has been developed by the office for the prevention of domestic violence in conjunction with the office of children and family services whose purpose is to develop an understanding of the dynamics of domestic violence and its connection to child abuse and neglect. Such course shall:

i   pay special attention to the need to screen for domestic violence;

    ii   place emphasis on the psychological harm experienced by children whose environment is impacted by familial violence and accordingly explore avenues to keep such children with the non-abusive parent rather than placing them in foster care further traumatizing both the victim and the children;

   iii provide instruction regarding the scope of legal remedies for the abused parent;

   iv identify obstacles that prevent individuals from leaving their batterers and examine safety options and services available for the victim;

    v provide information pertaining to the unique barriers facing certain immigrant women and the options available under the federal Violence Against Women Act … (NY CLS Soc. Serv. § 17)

Within this statute, "immigrant women" is an intersection of two status categories.

Discussion

Axes of Oppression and Impacts on Victim-Survivor Lives

The current chapter aimed to understand the extent to which state-level statutes are inclusive. This research question drew inspiration from the framework, intersectionality, which examines multiple intersecting inequalities—such as racism, sexism, and classism—as painting lived experience (see, e.g., Hill Collins & Bilge, 2020). While not in terms of intersections, state level statutes mentioned various statuses with experiences influenced by broader systems of inequality by discussing race, gender, and low-income (Ind. Code. Ann. 5-2-1-9; ALM GL ch. 12, Section 264). Indeed, statuses associated with these categories of analysis are salient in the lives of IMR victim-survivors of IPV. For example, a study of survivors and practitioners showed that formal sources of support may be viewed as less accessible than informal support sources because of prejudice based on race (Sabri et al., 2018). Silva-Martínez (2016) reported that racism was experienced in spaces that are quite important in IMR lives, such as the workplace.

    Along the axis of class (and accordingly, gender), in one study of immigrant Latinas, in addition to economic stress, economic challenges served as barriers to leaving an abusive relationship through lessened access to resources (Vidales, 2010). A study on Latina and

Caribbean immigrant women found that women faced backlash from violence-perpetrating partners when trying to improve their lives (Alvarez et al., 2021), a finding reminiscent of education and job sabotage that abusive partners employ against their partners (Raphael, 2000).

At the axis of gender, gender issues and inequality majorly shape experiences of abuse against IMR women (Alvarez et al., 2021; Kallivayalil, 2010; Reina, Maldonado, & Lohman, 2013; Ting, 2010; Vidales, 2010). In a study of immigrant Latinas, traditional gender role beliefs kept women tied to abuse, with men as entitled to hurt their spouses (Vidales, 2010). Ting's (2010) study of African immigrant IPV survivors found that women had to come to terms with their "fate" in the encompassing patriarchal culture. Reproductive issues are also salient in victim-survivors, such as forced pregnancies, as found in Kallivayalil's (2010) study on South Asian immigrant women. Mothering served as a site of both oppression and resistance in the context of abuse, such that while it was a reminder of putting ones needs second to others and how tied they were to their abusive partners (Kallivayalil, 2010), mothering was also a reminder of the importance of leaving abusive relationships and pursuing a better life (Alvarez et al., 2021).

Statutes and Inclusiveness

In trying to understand the inclusiveness of IMR-related IPV-related statutes, several other questions arise. First, what do we mean by inclusion? For this definition, we turn to Crenshaw's (1989) work:

> It is somewhat ironic that those concerned with alleviating the ills of racism and sexism should adopt such a top-down approach to discrimination. If their efforts instead began with addressing the needs and problems of those who are most disadvantaged and with restructuring and remaking the world where necessary, then others who are singularly disadvantaged would also benefit.
>
> (Crenshaw, 1989, p. 167)

In interpreting this statement, we believe that freeing people from oppression at the racism-sexism intersection not only frees people at said intersection but also other people who experience only racism or other people who experience only sexism. Thus, by inclusion, we mean freeing as many people as humanly possible.

Conclusion

Overall, state-level statutes that target IPV in IMR lives are generally *not* inclusive. Although some statutes list many statuses, they typically failed to state intersections. Among statutes that scattered their mentions of statuses and identities, there is even more conceptual distance between the stating of such statuses and the concept of inclusion. Among statutes that state intersections, there is no direct resource or service or protection provision (for a discussion of resources, see Coker, 2015; see also, Chapter 5). Instead, the intersections are locked up at the governmental or organizational level, running the risk of having a negligible impact on lived experiences of IMR IPV survivors of color, poor IMR IPV survivors, etc. Accordingly, we agree with McKinnon (2016) and critical race and feminist theorists that there is an "inability to see and hear intersectionally" within the law. However, it is less a matter of ability and more of a matter of will.

References

Alvarez, C., Lameiras-Fernandez, M., Holliday, C. N., Sabri, B., & Campbell, J. (2021). Latina and Caribbean immigrant women's experiences with intimate partner violence: A story of ambivalent sexism. *Journal of interpersonal violence*, *36*(7–8), 3831–3854.

BlackPast. (2012, November 16). (1977) The Combahee River Collective Statement. *BlackPast.org*. https://www.blackpast.org/african-american-history/combahee-river-collective-statement-1977/

Coker, D. (2005). Shifting power for battered women: Law, material resources, and poor women of color. In N. J. Sokoloff, & C. Pratt (Eds.), *Domestic violence at the margins: Readings on race, class, gender, and culture*. New Brunswick, NJ: Rutgers University Press.

Coker, D., & Macquoid, A. D. (2015). Why opposing hyper-incarceration should be central to the work of the domestic violence movement. *Miami Race & Social Justice Law Review*, 585–618.

Collins, P. H., & Bilge, S. (2020). *Intersectionality* (2nd ed.). Medford, MA: Polity Press.

Crenshaw, K. (1989). Demarginalizing the intersection of race and gender: A Black feminist critique of anti-discrimination doctrine, feminist theory, and anti-racist politics. *University of Chicago Legal Forum*, 139–167.

Crenshaw, K. (1991). Mapping the margins: Intersectionality, identity politics, and violence against women. *Stanford Law Review*, *43*(6), 1241–1299.

Crenshaw, K. W. (2013). From private violence to mass incarceration: Thinking intersectionally about women, race, and social control. *Journal of Scholarly Perspectives*, *9*(1), 23–50.

Kallivayalil, D. (2010). Narratives of suffering of South Asian immigrant survivors of domestic violence. *Violence against women, 16*(7), 789–811.

McKinnon, S. L. (2016). *Gendered asylum: Race and violence in U.S. law and politics* [Kindle version]. Urbana, Chicago, and Springfield, IL: University of Illinois Press.

Raphael, J. (2000). *Saving Bernice: Battered women, welfare, and poverty.* Northeastern University Press.

Reina, A. S., Maldonado, M. M., & Lohman, B. J. (2013). Undocumented Latina networks and responses to domestic violence in a new immigrant gateway: Toward a place-specific analysis. *Violence Against Women, 19*(12), 1472–1497.

Richie, B. E. (2015). Keynote—reimagining the movement to end gender violence: Anti-racism, prison abolition, women of color feminisms, and other radical visions of justice. *University of Miami Race & Social Justice Law Review*, 257–273.

Sabri, B., Nnawulezi, N., Njie-Carr, V. P. S., Messing, J., Ward-Lasher, A., Alvarez, C., & Campbell, J. C. (2018). Multilevel risk and protective factors for intimate partner violence among African, Asian, and Latina immigrant and refugee women: Perceptions of effective safety planning interventions. *Race and Social Problems, 10*, 348–365.

Silva-Martínez, E. (2016). "El silencio": Conceptualizations of Latina immigrant survivors of intimate partner violence in the Midwest of the United States. *Violence Against Women, 22*(5), 523–544.

Ting, L. (2010). Out of Africa: Coping strategies of African immigrant women survivors of intimate partner violence. *Health Care for Women International, 31*(4), 345–364.

Vidales, G. T. (2010). Arrested justice: The multifaceted plight of immigrant Latinas who faced domestic violence. *Journal of Family Violence, 25*, 533–544.

7 Cultivating Empathy

Empathy is a key human experience. In Harper Lee's book, *To Kill a Mockingbird*, character Atticus Finch discusses with his child the importance of taking another person's perspective: "You never really understand a person until you consider things from his point of view... Until you climb inside of his skin and walk around in it." Variations of this statement have been made throughout history, such as the long-standing idea of "walking in another person's shoes." This chapter applies the concept of empathy to the statutes. More specifically, the chapter aims to answer the following research question: To what extent do state-level statutes concerning IMR victim-survivors of IPV embody empathy? The chapter utilizes content analysis to see if state-level statutes mention/discuss the various hardships experienced by IPV-stricken IMR persons.

Empathy and Public Policy

Humans have a natural predisposition toward values like fairness, such as the idea that a person generally receives just reward and/or sanction for their deeds in life. However, when the balance of fairness tips toward a person receiving less than just treatment (e.g., false accusations of crimes, receiving lesser pay for diligent effort in the workplace), the fairness principle is violated, resulting in distress and catalyzing an empathic challenge to sources of injustice (Hoffman, 2011).

Counter to the widely held belief that there is a lack of consensus in defining empathy, a review of studies showed common themes regarding its definition:

- understanding;
- feeling;

DOI: 10.4324/9781003167044-7

- sharing; and
- grasping that others are separate from oneself.

Understanding is indicative of having some grasp of another person's mentality. Feeling, in this context, means that a person experiences an appropriate response to another person's situation. Sharing involves a person experiencing situations in cohesion to the way another person experiences a situation. Self-other differentiation involves grasping that another person is a separate being from oneself, like a boundary (Eklund & Meranius, 2020).

Hoffman (2011) defines empathy "as an emotional state triggered by another's emotional state or situation, in which one feels what the other feels ..." (p. 231). An important aspect of empathy is perspective-taking. Hoffman (2011) discussed how the process and outcome of the landmark court case, *Brown v. Board of Education* (1954), exhibited empathy. In the process, Thurgood Marshall deviated from traditional means of arguing court cases by painting a multi-part picture of Black children's experiences in segregation, using terms like "inferiority," as well as Black children's internalization of racist attitudes through discussing a study on dolls that exposed their "self-hatred." In their decision, the Court stated that:

> The impact is greater when it has the sanction of law, for the policy of separating the races is usually interpreted as denoting the inferiority of the Negro group. A sense of inferiority affects the motivation of the child to learn. Segregation with the sanction of law therefore has a tendency to [retard] the educational and mental development of Negro children.
> (Brown v. Board, as cited in Hoffman, 2011, p. 247)

The usage of terms such as "inferiority" and acknowledging negative impacts on learning, educational and mental development partially engrained the hardship and injustice experienced by Black children into a formal judicial output.

In Chapter 5, we drew on the work of Smith (2005, 1997) to discuss how people's standpoints and views are collectivized to change text and, by extension, ruling relations that impact individuals' lived experiences. Looking empirically, while the nature of the relationship may depend on the meaningfulness of the public's opinions on certain policies, the opinion-policy relationship is generally statistically significant; that is, studies show that certain policies are more likely to be adopted when support for such policies is at an increased level;

however, this relationship is nuanced and allows for other sources of policy development to be in play as well (see, e.g., Burstein, 2003, 2006; Lax & Phillips, 2009). When looking at a gallery of policies and services (e.g., warrantless arrest, funding for domestic violence shelters, state efforts on violence against women of color), Weldon (2006) found that organizing by women of color was significantly related to the strength of the population-adjusted number of women's organizations, as well as indirectly related to how much the state addressed violence against women.

Regardless of the patchwork of ways through which they are created, laws are ultimately made by humans. It would make sense that aspects of the human experience, including empathy, would seep into human-made creations. When texts giving life to injustice are challenged, humans' empathic distress may be etched into new laws that challenge the pre-existing legal structures sanctioning inequality. In codifying solutions to extant issues and injustice, acknowledgment of struggles, plights, and hardships of certain groups may also be codified into the legal texts. To understand if and how state-level statutes etch the perspective-taking aspect of human empathy into the legal structure, the present research looks at whether statutes mention various issues that specifically target IMR victim-survivors of IPV.

Empathy and Statutes

About 44 percent ($n = 32$) of statutes, in some way, mentioned issues that specifically affect IPV in IMR victim-survivors' lives. While no statutes addressed social isolation and economic dependence on violence-perpetrating partners, others mentioned deportation/removal, language barriers, gender norms, and various other sub-topics (see Table 7.1).

Deportation/Removal

About forty-one percent of issue-mentioning statutes ($n = 13$) mentioned, in some way, deportation/removal. For example, Section 679.10 of the California Penal Code states, in setting forth the definition and functioning of certifying entities for U nonimmigrant status, in part expedites the process of processing the U nonimmigrant visa supporting documentation, specifically if the person filing is in removal proceedings

Table 7.1 Issues in the Lives of Immigrant and Refugee Victim-Survivors of Intimate Partner Violence ($N = 32/72$)

Category	n	%
Isolation	0	0
Deportation/Removal	13	40.63
Economic Dependence on Partner	0	0
Language Barrier	2	6.25
Gender Norms	1	3.13
Other Topics[a]	16	50.00

Note:

a The following statutes were categorized under the "Other Topics" category: Cal Gov Code § 13963.1, Cal Gov Code § 13963.2, Cal Pen Code § 13823.17, ALM GL ch. 12, § 33, ALM GL ch. 112, § 264, NY CLS CPL § 530.12, NY CLS Dom Rel § 252, NY CLS Fam Ct Act § 446, NY CLS Fam Ct Act § 551, NY CLS Fam Ct Act § 842, NY CLS Fam Ct Act § 1056, NY CLS Soc Serv § 17, Rev. Code Wash. § 7.98.005, Cal. Wel. & Inst. Code § 13305, 305 ILCS 5/16-1, and 305 ILCS 5/16-4.

A certifying entity shall process a Form I-918 Supplement B certification within 30 days of request, unless the noncitizen is in removal proceedings, in which case the certification shall be processed within 7 days of the first business day following the day the request was received.

(Cal Pen Code 679.10)

In another example, Section 239B.2B of the Iowa Code states that:

A person who meets the conditions of eligibility under section 239B.2 and who meets either of the following requirements shall be eligible for participation in the family investment program:

1 The person is a conditional resident alien who was battered or subjected to extreme cruelty, or whose child was battered or subjected to extreme cruelty, perpetrated by the person's spouse who is a United States citizen or lawful permanent resident as described in 8 C.F.R. § 216.5(a)(3).
2 The person was battered or subjected to extreme cruelty, or the person's child was battered or subjected to extreme cruelty, perpetrated by the person's spouse who is a United States citizen or lawful permanent resident and the person's petition

has been approved or a petition is pending that sets forth a prima facie case that the person has noncitizen status under any of the following categories:

a   Status as a spouse or child of a United States citizen or lawful permanent resident under the federal Immigration and Nationality Act, §204(a)(1), as codified in 8 U.S.C. §1154(a)(1)(A).

b   Status as a spouse or child who was battered or subjected to extreme cruelty by a United States citizen or lawful permanent resident, under the federal Immigration and Nationality Act, §204(a)(iii), as codified in 8 U.S.C. §1154(a)(1)(A)(iii).

c   Classification as a person lawfully admitted for permanent residence under the federal Immigration and Nationality Act.

d   Suspension of deportation and adjustment of status under the federal Immigration and Nationality Act, §244(a), as in effect before the date of enactment of the federal Illegal Immigration Reform and Immigrant Responsibility Act of 1996.

e   Cancellation of removal or adjustment of status under the federal Immigration and Nationality Act, §240A, as codified in 8 U.S.C. §1229b.

f   Status as an asylee, if asylum is pending, under the federal Immigration and Nationality Act, §208, as codified in 8 U.S.C. §1158. (Iowa Code § 239B.2B).

Language Barrier

Approximately, six percent of issue-mentioning statutes ($n = 2$) mentioned, in some way, language barriers. For example, Section 13303 of the California Welfare and Institutions Code states, in part, the following:

(a) (e) The department shall update the Legislature on the following information in the course of budget hearings:

1   The timeline for implementation and administration of this section, including important upcoming dates.

2   The participating organizations awarded contracts or grants, and the aggregate amounts awarded for each service described in subdivision (b).

3 The number of applications submitted, and the aggregate amounts requested for each service described in subdivision (b).
4 The number of clients served.
5 The types of services provided and in what language or languages.
6 The regions served.
7 The ethnic communities served.
8 The identification of further barriers and challenges to the provision of services... (Cal. Wel. & Inst. § Code 13303)

In discussing certifying agencies, the Revised Code of Washington states that "All certifying agencies shall develop a language access protocol for limited English proficient and deaf or hard of hearing victims of criminal activity" (Rev. Code Wash. § 7.98.010).

Gender Norms

One statute (approximately 3 percent), in some way, regarded gender norms. Section 13823.17 of the California Penal Code states, in part, as follows:

a The Legislature finds the problem of domestic violence in the gay, lesbian, bisexual, and transgender community to be of serious and increasing magnitude. The Legislature also finds that existing domestic violence services for this population are underfunded and that members of this population are unserved or underserved in the state. Therefore, it is the intent of the Legislature that a goal of the Office of Emergency Services shall be to increase access to domestic violence education, prevention, and services specifically for the gay, lesbian, bisexual, and transgender community.

This statute was coded as one that concerns gender norms because of its inclusion of the transgender community.

Other Topics

Fifty percent of issue-mentioning statutes ($n = 16$) mentioned hardships best coded under an "Other" category. Some statutes dealt with the effects of violence. For example, Section 13963.1 of the California Government Code sets forth criteria by which the state will determine grant provision for trauma recovery centers purposed to mitigate psychological trauma:

The board, when considering grant applications, shall give preference to a trauma recovery center that conducts outreach to, both of the following: Crime victims who are typically unable to access traditional services, including ... members of immigrant and refugee groups...[and] Victims of a wide range of crimes, including, but not limited to, victims of sexual assault, domestic violence, physical assault, shooting, stabbing, human trafficking, and vehicular assault, and family members of homicide victims.

(Cal Gov Code § 13963.1)

This statute also acknowledges the hurt and pain of victims, etching the potential perspective of IMR IPV survivors in multiple ways. First, the statute acknowledges the psychological pain that victims can experience: "untreated psychological trauma often has severe economic consequences" (Cal Gov Code 13963.1). Moreover, it acknowledges the potential for domestic violence victims who are members of immigrant and refugee groups to "typically [be] unable to access traditional services" (Cal Gov Code 13963.1). Here, the statute possesses an understanding of the issues faced by such a group and various constellations of other disaffected communities. Section 13963.2 of the California Government Code integrates an actionable component to activate the perspective-taking; specifically, the statute states that trauma recovery centers must provide outreach, offer evidence-based mental health and support services, as well as support other developments like "promoting post-traumatic growth."

Some statutes regulate and attempt to mitigate specific violent tactics. In a series of statutes concerning protection orders, New York pinpoints the issue of IMR IPV victim-survivors having their identification documents stolen by violence-perpetrating partners. Section 842 of the Family Court Act in the New York Consolidated Laws states that persons should

promptly return specified identification documents to the protected party, in whose favor the order of protection or temporary order of protection is issued ... "identification document" shall mean any of the following: ... birth certificate, passport, social security card, health insurance or other benefits card, a card or document used to access bank, credit or other financial accounts or records, tax returns, any driver's license, and immigration documents including but not limited to a United States permanent resident card and employment authorization document ...

(NY CLS Fam Ct Act § 842)

One statute from Washington acknowledged IMR IPV victim-survivors' complicated relationship with the State.

> The legislature finds that ensuring that all victims of crimes are able to access the protections available to them under law is in the best interest of victims, law enforcement, and the entire community. Immigrants are frequently reluctant to cooperate with or contact law enforcement when they are victims of crimes, and the protections available to immigrants under the law are designed to strengthen the ability of law enforcement agencies to detect, investigate, and prosecute cases of trafficking in persons, domestic violence, sexual assault, and other crimes while offering protection to such victims.
>
> (Wash. Rev. Code § 7.98.005)

This statute, while symbolic, acknowledges the reluctance of immigrant victim-survivors to ask for help from formal authorities.

A statute from Massachusetts targeted law enforcement/criminal justice as a subject, specifically focusing on administrative training regarding domestic violence for district attorneys and assistant district attorneys.

> The Massachusetts District Attorneys' Association shall provide training on the issue of domestic violence and sexual violence in the commonwealth, at least once biannually, to all district attorneys and assistant district attorneys. Such training shall include, but not be limited to, the dissemination of information concerning:
>
> 1 misdemeanor and felony offenses in which domestic violence and sexual violence are often involved;
> 2 the civil rights and remedies available to victims of domestic violence and sexual violence;
> 3 methods for assessing the degree of risk of homicide involved in situations of domestic violence including, but not limited to, gathering information from the victim regarding the suspect's past reported and non-reported behavior and dangerousness, such as: (i) whether the suspect has ever used a weapon against the victim or threatened the victim with a weapon; (ii) whether the suspect owns a gun; (iii) whether the suspect's physical violence against the victim has increased in severity or frequency; (iv) whether the suspect has threatened to kill the victim; (v) whether the suspect has ever threatened

or attempted suicide; (vi) whether the suspect has used or threatened physical violence against the victim's family, other household members or pets; (vii) whether the suspect uses illegal drugs; (viii) whether the suspect abuses alcohol; and (ix) whether there have been specific instances of strangulation or suffocation of the victim by the suspect;

4 law enforcement techniques, information sharing and methods of promoting cooperation among different areas of law enforcement in combating domestic violence and sexual violence, including the importance of keeping victims informed as to the whereabouts of suspected abusers and other such information helpful for victim safety planning;

5 the physiological and psychological effects of the pattern of domestic violence and sexual violence on its victims, including children who witness such abuse;

6 the increased vulnerability of victims who are gay, lesbian, bisexual, transgender, low-income, minority or immigrant, and including training on ways in which the indicators of dangerousness in these communities may be different from those in non-marginalized communities;

7 the dynamics of coercive controlling behavior that increases dangerousness even when such patterns of behavior are not themselves violent;

8 the underlying psychological and sociological causes of domestic violence and sexual violence and the availability of batterer's intervention programs;

9 the availability of community based domestic violence, rape, and sexual assault shelter and support services within the commonwealth, including, to the extent practicable, specific shelter and support services available in a district attorney's district; and

10 techniques for increasing cooperation and immediate data sharing among different areas of law enforcement and the court system in combating domestic violence and sexual violence.

The Massachusetts District Attorneys' Association may appoint such expert, clerical and other staff members as the operation of the training program may require. As appropriate, the training presenters shall include domestic violence and sexual violence experts with expertise in the delivery of direct services to victims of domestic violence and sexual violence, including utilizing community based domestic violence, rape and sexual assault service providers and survivors of domestic violence, rape or sexual assault in the presentation of the training.

(ALM GL ch. 12, § 33)

A part of this statute mentions "increased vulnerability" for a series of classes, statuses, and identities. Moreover, it juxtaposes their experiences of dangerousness to "non-marginalized communities," meaning that the statute intends to frame certain groups as marginalized.

Discussion

Over 40 percent of state-level statutes targeting IPV in IMR lives discussed issues that commonly affect victim-survivors. Statutes used aspects of empathy such as perspective-taking, understanding, etc., to spotlight victim-survivors' various hardships and unique situations. Many statutes that mentioned issues affecting IMR IPV survivors seem responsive to the specific issues targeting this population of victims. For example, two statutes discussed language barriers. Language barriers are a particularly salient barrier to accessing help for IMR victim-survivors of IPV (Latta & Goodman, 2005; Reina, Lohman, & Maldonado, 2014; Silva-Martínez, 2016; Shiu-Thornton et al., 2005; Silva-Martínez, 2016). Silva-Martínez (2016) and Vidales (2010) show that these barriers can result in feelings of frustration, powerlessness, and worthlessness. In addition to not being able to communicate needs to service providers and authorities, there is also the potential for difficulty talking to law enforcement.

As seen in the statutes that noted deportation/removal and reluctance to contact law enforcement (e.g., Wash. Rev. Code § 7.98.005), there is a dissonance that pins IMR IPV victim-survivors between violence-perpetrating partners and the immigration/policing system that sows distrust and fear. Indeed, immigrant women who experience IPV may fear having their children taken away by authorities (Erez, Adelman, & Gregory, 2009; Kelly, 2009; Salcido & Adelman, 2004; Silva-Martínez, 2015; Vidales, 2010). In Kelly's (2009) work, immigrant survivors did their best to stop word or signs of abuse from leaving the house and garnering the attention of authorities, which:

> could separate them from their children by loss of custody or deportation, leaving their children without the love and protection of their mothers. They believed that CPS would take custody of their children based on the assumption that if a mother is being abused, so are her children, or that mothers who remain with abusers are failing to protect their children from witnessing

abuse, and are therefore neglectful or abusive themselves. Many of the women viewed CPS as more dangerous to their children than the abuser.

(p. 293)

It is also well-researched that some IMR victim-survivors of IPV may be worried about potential removal from the U.S. (Latta & Goodman, 2005; Mahapatra & Rai, 2019; Reina et al., 2014; Silva-Martínez, 2015; Salcido & Adelman, 2004).

The mention of marginalization in Massachusetts's legal structure opens the opportunity to discuss marginalization more broadly. One of Massachusetts' statutes lists a series of statuses (e.g., minority, transgender), then compares them to "non-marginalized" statuses (ALM GL ch. 12, § 33). Positioned in relation to a center, people who do not fit within the descriptive boundaries of such a center are pushed toward a margin, in which they become the Other. Exclusion and being pushed toward the margins are defined based on characteristics ascribed to the person experiencing marginalization. To add insult to injury, "borderlands" exist, whereby people inhabit the space that exists between two or more margins, fortifying their Otherness (Vasas, 2005). In the context of these descriptions, "Marginalized populations ... are groups of people who are socially excluded and experience inequalities in the distribution of resources of power" (Vasas, 2005, p. 195).

Some studying law has, for a long time, thought that the law replaces emotion with logic, while others believe that what humans feel sneaks into law (Hoffman, 2011). The present analysis provides some support for the latter statement. Does empathy matter? As Hoffman (2011) states, "It can have an impact on making laws and on creating the social and emotional climate and support for changing them, as well as on the practice of implementing them in the courtroom" (Hoffman, 2011, p. 253). In creating laws, people may etch pieces of the human experience—like empathy—into the textual structures that demarcate the boundaries of human and governmental behavior.

Conclusion

This chapter's analysis showed statutes discussed many issues targeting IPV in IMR lives, such as trauma, removal, marginalization, language barriers, and reluctance to engage with law enforcement. Overall, statutes show that law itself does not have to be a cold, hardened construct, but rather something that balances considering human experience with standard benchmarks for ensuring justice.

References

Burstein, P. (2003). The impact of public opinion on public policy: A review and an agenda. *Political Research Quarterly*, *56*(1), 29–40.

Burstein, P. (2006). Why estimates of the impact of public opinion on public policy are too high: Empirical and theoretical implications. *Social Forces*, *84*(4), 2273–2289.

Eklund, J. H., & Meranius, M. S. (2020). Toward a consensus on the nature of empathy: A review of reviews. *Patient Education and Counseling*, *104*(2), 300–307.

Hoffman, M. L. (2011). Empathy, justice, and the law. In A. Coplan, & P. Goldie (Eds.), *Empathy: Philosophical and psychological perspectives*. Oxford, UK: Oxford University Press.

Latta, R. E., & Goodman, L. A. (2005). Considering the interplay of cultural context and service provision in intimate partner violence: The case of Haitian immigrant women. *Violence Against Women*, *11*(11), 1441–1464.

Lax, J. R., & Phillips, J. H. (2009). Gay rights in the states: Public opinion and policy responsiveness. *American Political Science Review*, *103*(3), 367–386.

Mahapatra, N., & Rai, A. (2019). "Every cloud has a silver lining but…": Pathways to seeking formal-help and South-Asian immigrant women survivors of intimate partner violence". *Health Care for Women International*, *40*(11), 1170–1196.

Reina, A. S., Lohman, B. J., & Maldonado, M. M. (2014). "He said they'd deport me": Factors influencing domestic violence help-seeking practices among Latina immigrants. *Journal of Interpersonal Violence*, *29*(4), 593–615.

Salcido, O., & Adelman, M. (2004). "He has me tied with the blessed and damned papers": Undocumented-immigrant battered women in Phoenix, Arizona. *Human Organization*, 162–172.

Shiu-Thornton, S., Senturia, K., & Sullivan, M. (2005). "Like a bird in a cage": Vietnamese women survivors talk about domestic violence. *Journal of Interpersonal Violence*, *20*(8), 959–976.

Silva-Martínez, E. (2016). "El Silencio" conceptualizations of Latina immigrant survivors of intimate partner violence in the Midwest of the United States. *Violence Against Women*, *22*(5), 523–544.

Smith, D. (2005). Institutional ethnography. In S. Appelrouth, & L. D. Edles (Eds.), *Classical and contemporary sociological theory: Text and readings* (pp. 591–602). Thousand Oaks, CA: Pine Forge Press.

Smith, D. E. (1997). Consciousness, meaning, and ruling relations: From women's standpoint. In *Millennial milestone: The heritage and future of sociology in the North American region*. Toronto, Canada: Proceedings of the ISA Regional Conference for North America (pp. 37–50).

Vidales, G. T. (2010). Arrested justice: The multifaceted plight of immigrant Latinas who faced domestic violence. *Journal of Family Violence, 25*(6), 533–544.

Weldon, S. L. (2006). Women's movements, identity politics, and policy impacts: A study of policies on violence against women in the 50 United States. *Political Research Quarterly*, *59*(1), 111–122.

8 Shifting Power

Empowerment is an important cornerstone of the movement to end domestic violence. This chapter applies the concept of empowerment to state-level statutes targeting IPV in IMR lives. This chapter provides an overview of the concept of empowerment, including its history in the domestic violence movement, the salience of power in abusive relationships, and empowerment to escape IPV. In relation to statutes, empowerment is operationalized at the structural level as the shifting (or displacement) of resources. A discussion of findings examining empowerment within statutes is provided, showing that there are limits to the extent that statutes provide direct resource support to victim-survivors.

Empowerment

The genesis of the shelter movement featured a grassroots effort by women of various backgrounds. This movement was an afront to the patriarchal organization of society that laid the foundation upon which abuse occurs. In addition to needing to gain consciousness of these dynamics, it was put forth that battered women "needed ultimately to be 'empowered'—that is mobilized to challenge their subjection and take charge of their lives (Penz, 1981)" (Gondolf & Fisher, 1988, p. 1). Empowerment was a clear goal of the movement against domestic violence (Cattaneo & Goodman, 2015; Gondolf & Fisher, 1988).

The term *power* has its place in the extant literature concerning IPV. The Power and Control Wheel depicts power and control as central motivations that give rise to various non-physical tactics (e.g., instilling fear through specific looks and gestures, controlling the ability to communicate with other people), which perpetuate the perpetration of physical and/or sexual violence against a victim-survivor (Pence & Paymar, 1993). In a related example, Johnson's (2008) work on

DOI: 10.4324/9781003167044-8

distinctions among configurations of IPV found that there are a number of ways violence manifests in intimate dyads:

- via situational couple violence (roughly gender symmetric, less likely to be severe, and with low levels of control);
- via intimate terrorism[1] (overwhelmingly male-perpetrated, more likely to be severe and result in injury, and high levels of control);
- via violent resistance (overwhelmingly female-perpetrated, non-controlling, and resembles self-defense).

In this context, the term intimate terrorism itself is characterized as a "powerful combination of violence with a general pattern of control," which "is terrorizing because once a controlling partner has been violent, all of his other controlling actions take on the threat of violence" (Johnson, 2008, p. 26).

There are various manifestations of power within the extant literature (e.g., "power over," "power to," "power from"; see Riger, 1993). Power can be defined broadly as "one's influence in social relations" (Cattaneo & Chapman, 2010, p. 647). It would seem that in a controllingly violent relationship, a victim-survivor's influence would be lower in the power relationship between two people in an intimate dyad. This is where empowerment becomes salient. Empowerment features "a meaningful shift in the experience of power attained through interaction with the social world" (Cattaneo & Goodman, 2015, p. 84). Thus, empowerment occurs in IPV when a victim-survivor changes or has the opportunity to change their subjugated position within a violent relationship and/or the social world around them as a means to reclaim freedom from IPV.

In describing the empowerment process model, Cattaneo and Chapman (2010) discuss the story of Sara, an undocumented IPV victim-survivor. Sara's husband, a U.S. citizen, physically assaulted her and used deportation as a tool to threaten her. In one violent episode against Sara, the police were called and arrested her husband. Sara became very worried that her undocumented status would be discovered. Accordingly, she became intent on dropping the charges and devising a way to keep her immigration status concealed. Cattaneo and Chapman show that, while interacting with the system, advocates, neighbors, and her abusive partner, Sara's position changes as she thinks through engaging with the legal system. In a couple of parts of her story, Sara gains knowledge that she uses to refine her goal and take further action.

Sarah's story shows a journey through the empowerment process, as well as how it is impacted by and changes in relation to other actors and systems. But, moreover, Cattaneo and Chapman (2010) hypothesize that an advocate working with Sara could "conclude that policy changes were needed in order to create other options for such women" (e.g., VAWA's IMR-related provisions; p. 655). Policy changes may be particularly salient in terms of empowerment because they hold the promise of adding more pathways though which victim-survivors can venture. Indeed, as Gondolf and Fisher (1988) argue, abuse victim-survivors are often not passive people who have learned helplessness, but rather are active help-seekers that a system fails time and time again. Accordingly, there may be importance in continuing to shift attention from whether victim-survivors are *empowered* to whether the system is *empowering*. Victim-survivors' "first step" (Smith, 2001) must be met with "a helping hand" from the State (Orloff & Kagayutan, 2002).

In this context, we follow Cattaneo and Goodman's (2015) conceptualization of empowerment, specifically its "meaningful shift in the experience of power" (Cattaneo & Goodman, 2015, p. 84). In terms of power, since we are working with government, politics, and policy, we define power in terms of resources. To operationalize empowerment, we define its presence in relation to statutes as the shifting (or displacement) of resources, as told by the statutes and as seen by the coders.

Empowerment and Statutes

About 11 percent ($n = 8$) of statutes were coded as shifting resources. Statutes shifted resources in ways such as

- from government (as well as perpetrators) to social services;
- from government to victim-survivors (see Figure 8.1).

For example, flowing from government to social services, Section 13303 of the California Welfare and Institutions Code provides grant funding to organizations that help with immigration remedies (e.g., VAWA self-petitions):

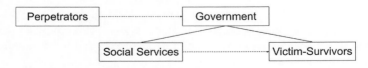

Figure 8.1 Direction of resource transfer among state-level statutes.

a Subject to the availability of funding in the act that added this section or the annual Budget Act, the department shall provide grants, as described in subdivision (b), to organizations qualified under Section 13304.

b Grants provided in accordance with subdivision (a) shall be for the purpose of providing one or more of the following services, as determined by the department...

(A) (B) Services to obtain other immigration remedies...(4) "Immigration remedies" include, but shall not be limited to, U-visas, T-visas, special immigrant juvenile status, Violence Against Women Act self-petitions, family-based petitions, cancellation of removal, and asylum, or other remedies that may also include remedies necessary to enable pursuit of immigration protections. (Cal Wel. & Inst. Code § 13303)

Section 1463.27 of the California Penal Code levies a 250-dollar fine against domestic violence perpetrators, transferring such funds to domestic violence programs that service immigrant, refugee, and rural populations:

a Notwithstanding any other provision of law, in addition to any other fine or penalty assessment, the board of supervisors of a county may, by resolution, authorize a fee of not more than two hundred fifty dollars ($250) upon every fine, penalty, or forfeiture imposed and collected by the courts for a crime of domestic violence specified in paragraph (1) of subdivision (c) of Section 243 and in Section 273.5. Notwithstanding Section 1463 or 1464, money collected pursuant to this section shall be used to fund domestic violence prevention programs that focus on assisting immigrants, refugees, or persons who live in a rural community. Counties with existing domestic violence prevention programs that assist those persons may direct funds to those programs.

b The court shall determine if the defendant has the ability to pay the fee imposed under this section. In making that determination, the court shall take into account the total amount of fines and restitution that the defendant is subject to, and may waive payment of this additional fee.

c The court shall deposit the moneys collected pursuant to this section in a fund designated by the board of supervisors, to be used as specified in subdivision (a).

(Cal Pen Code § 1463.27)

In this context, resources flow from perpetrators to government to social services.

As another example, transmitting resources from government to victim-survivors, Section 5/16-1 of Title 305 of the Illinois Consolidated Statutes allows for cash and food assistance for foreign-born victims of serious crimes and torture, granted that they meet eligibility criteria (e.g., filing for U nonimmigrant status:

> A foreign-born victim of trafficking, torture, or other serious crimes and his or her derivative family members are eligible for cash assistance or SNAP benefits under this Article if: (a) he or she: (1) has filed or is preparing to file an application for T Nonimmigrant status with the appropriate federal agency pursuant to Section 1101(a)(15)(T) of Title 8 of the United States Code, or is otherwise taking steps to meet the conditions for federal benefits eligibility under Section 7105 of Title 22 of the United States Code; (2) has filed or is preparing to file a formal application with the appropriate federal agency for status pursuant to Section 1101(a)(15)(U) of Title 8 of the United States Code; or (3) has filed or is preparing to file a formal application with the appropriate federal agency for status under Section 1158 of Title 8 of the United States Code; and (b) he or she is otherwise eligible for cash assistance or SNAP benefits, as applicable.
>
> (305 ILCS 5/16-2)

The statute also shows that resource shifts occur within the government as well, such as a provision that uses state-level funds for such assistance if federal-level funds are unavailable.

Discussion

In this chapter, we found that a small number (approximately 11 percent) of statutes shifted resources, generally from government to either social services or victim-survivors. However, as we see next, the direct shifting of resources to victims is limited within these laws. This means that there are limits as to the empowering potentials of state-level laws targeting IPV against IMR persons.

In Coker's (2002) analysis, it is put forth that the "potential risks of arrest must be examined in determining whether arrest encouraging policies are likely to, on balance, enhance access to material resources for women of color" (p. 381). Coker (2002) then applies this analysis to the risk of deportation, in which the major 1996 immigration overhaul spelled danger for IMR victim-survivors who self-defend. The analysis tells the story of Maria Sanchez, who engaged in self-defense against her abusive husband. From a variety of factors (her husband's calling the police, a language barrier blocking her from telling her side of the story), Maria faced deportation because she was arrested and convicted in the context of the violent episode (Coker, 2002). In this context, an arrest-enhancing approach to battering may cause so much damage to victim-survivors that any benefit is outweighed by the costs. Thus, an approach that centers victim-survivors through shifting material resources directly to them would be of more service than an arrest-encouraging policy (see Coker, 2002). This sentiment has been echoed by Goodmark (2018), who takes a victim-centered approach to IPV policy, that is, by arguing against the usage of criminalization as the primary method to deal with violence and instead supplanting much of the criminalization agenda (except, e.g., focusing on the most dangerous offenders) with resource-enhancing and community-driven approaches.

In application, the Illinois statute discussed earlier in this chapter conditioned the obtaining of cash assistance or SNAP on applying for or obtaining status under Section 1101(a)(15)(U) of Title 8 of the United States Code (U Non-immigrant status; 305 ILCS 5/16-2). Here, there is a synthesis of criminalization (i.e., that the U-visa is used to investigate crimes) and direct resource allocation (i.e., that benefits are offered directly from the government to the victim-survivor). However, the trade-off within this statute (see also Chapter 4) mitigates its directness in providing benefits (i.e., resources to survivors) because there is a mediating step. These dynamics further mitigate the empowering potential of the law. At the same time, U Non-immigrant status is accompanied by protection from removal, which makes a clearer pathway to protection from the State. This becomes salient in the context of the victim-survivors' social power in relation to the violence perpetrating partner. The statute seems empowering and disempowering at the same time.

Conclusion

This chapter applied the construct, empowerment, to state-level statutes targeting IPV in IMR lives. It operationalized empowerment as power shifting (see Cattaneo & Goodman, 2015), or more specifically, resource shifting. Only a small fraction of statutes shifted resources. Fewer offered direct transfer routes between resource sources and victim-survivors. Analyzing a statute through the lens advocating for direct resource provision to survivors revealed that the empowering potential of law may be complex.

Note

1. *Intimate terrorism* is also known as *coercive controlling violence* (Kelly & Johnson, 2008).

References

Cattaneo, L. B., & Chapman, A. R. (2010). The process of empowerment: A model for use in research and practice. *American Psychologist*, *65*(7), 646–659.

Cattaneo, L. B., & Goodman, L. A. (2015). What is empowerment anyway? A model for domestic violence practice, research, and evaluation. *Psychology of Violence*, *5*(1), 84–94.

Coker, D. (2002). Shifting power for battered women: Law, material resources, and poor women of color. In N. J. Sokoloff, & C. Pratt (Eds.), *Domestic violence at the margins: Readings on race, class, gender, and culture.* New Brunswick, NJ: Rutgers University Press.

Gondolf, E. W., & Fisher, E. R. (1988). *Battered women as survivors: An alternative to treating learned helplessness.* Massachusetts, MA: Lexington Books.

Goodmark, L. (2018). *Decriminalizing domestic violence: A balanced policy approach to intimate partner violence.* Oakland, CA: University of California Press.

Johnson, M. P. (2008). *A typology of domestic violence: Intimate terrorism, violent resistance, and situational couple violence.* Boston, MA: Northeastern University Press.

Kelly, J. B., & Johnson, M. P. (2008). Differentiation among types of intimate partner violence: Research update and implications for interventions. *Family Court Review*, *46*(3), 476–499. https://doi.org/10.1111/j.1744-1617.2008.00215.x.

Orloff, L. E., & Kagayutan, J. V. (2002). Offering a helping hand: Legal protections for battered immigrant women: A history of legislative responses. *American University Journal of Gender, Social Policy, and the Law*, *10*(1), 95–170.

Pence, E., & Paymar, M. (1993). Education groups for men who batter: The Duluth model. New York, NY: Springer Publishing Company, Inc.

Riger, S. (1993). What's wrong with empowerment. *American Journal of Community Psychology*, *21*(3), 279–292.

Smith, A. (2001). Domestic violence laws: The voices of battered women. *Violence & Victims*, *16*(1), 91–111.

9 Shaping Status

This chapter answers the following research question: How do state-level statutes shape the status of IMR victim-survivors of IPV? First, the present research draws on phenomena across certain variables (i.e., social control, empathy, empowerment, and identity terms) from the analyses of previous chapters. Next, through the synthesis of quantitative data within these categories, we discuss how certain characteristics shape the status of IMR victim-survivors of IPV.

Stratification and Status

According to Massey (2007), humans place other humans into categories. These categories are then constructed and reproduced. In the process of creating categories, human beings convince others to agree to the legitimacy of such categories through framing. When framing is employed by people in power, the corresponding categories are more likely to be deemed legitimate. In this context, when applied to many individuals, categories give rise to social identities, which are segmented into in-groups and out-groups based on varying degrees of perceived competence and warmth. When out-groups are perceived as incompetent and cold, such groups become despised, triggering perceptions of being inhuman and setting the stage for exploitation to take shape. The application of labels solidifies perceived differences among and between groups. Resources are then either taken from the out-group or monopolized by the in-group. These dynamics become reproduced in various social settings, becoming instilled in such a way as to pervasively perpetuate the resulting system of stratification (Massey, 2007).

Under the conditions of stratification, an individual has a status, or a "specific, positive or negative, social estimation of *honor*" (Weber, 1925/2008, p. 170), which can be imposed by formal or informal means

DOI: 10.4324/9781003167044-9

(e.g., via law versus religious practice). Status, in addition to possibly being associated with class, comes in the form of stubborn variation in the allocation of life experiences like belonging (Weber, 1925/2008). For example, in 1968, an elementary school teacher named Jane Elliot conducted an exercise with her students in which she divided the students into groups of those with blue eyes and those with brown eyes. Throughout the school day, the teacher gave privileges and positive praise to one eye-color group, while withholding them from the other group. The teacher repeated the exercise again with the opposite group in the privileged position. The teacher reported greater behavioral and educational differences between the groups based on which group did not receive privileges and positive praise (Elliot, n.d.; PBS, 2003). In this case, a greater social honor was bestowed upon one group, and resources (e.g., privileges) were allocated accordingly.

Stratification within the U.S. is based on various factors (e.g., race, class, gender, sexuality, ability), with race, class, and gender intertwining to make the outcomes of stratification complex (see, e.g., Crenshaw, 1989; Collins & Bilge, 2020). Thus, social honor—status—is bestowed in complex ways. To understand the status of IMR persons affected by IPV, we draw from previous chapters to discuss how the legal system plays a role in shaping the raced and gendered social honors that are bestowed upon such individuals. In order to do so, we also look at class as an economic version of stubborn social honor variation which is contextualized politically (see Weber, 1925/2008).

Statutes and Status Construction

In previous chapters, we looked at how statutes mentioned or addressed federal policies and labels (Chapter 3), surveillance and social control (Chapter 4), resources (Chapter 5), demographics (Chapter 6), empathy (Chapter 7), and empowerment (Chapter 8). However, what do our findings say or not say about the social honor of IMR victim-survivors of IPV?

First, approximately 33 percent of statutes instituted requirements to secure protection or benefits (see Chapter 4). While the protections themselves may be helpful in relation to the overarching restrictionism of the U.S. immigration system, indeed, they are still a piece of the overarching structure. By interrogating the political and economic aspects and implications of such a statute characteristic, we can expose and discuss the social aspect. It would seem that, although we cannot stress enough the helpful and protective nature of the statute in relation to more restrictionist policies that exist, the State uses victim-survivors as "tools" to meet carceral ends. For example, the Illinois Compiled Statutes states as follows:

> A foreign-born victim of trafficking, torture, or other serious crimes and his or her derivative family members are eligible for cash assistance or SNAP benefits under this Article if: (a) he or she: (1) has filed or is preparing to file an application for T Nonimmigrant status with the appropriate federal agency pursuant to Section 1101(a)(15)(T) of Title 8 of the United States Code, or is otherwise taking steps to meet the conditions for federal benefits eligibility under Section 7105 of Title 22 of the United States Code; (2) has filed or is preparing to file a formal application with the appropriate federal agency for status pursuant to Section 1101(a)(15)(U) of Title 8 of the United States Code; or (3) has filed or is preparing to file a formal application with the appropriate federal agency for status under Section 1158 of Title 8 of the United States Code; and (b) he or she is otherwise eligible for cash assistance or SNAP benefits, as applicable.
>
> (305 ILCS 5/16-2)

In this case, the statute hints at class by listing cash and food public benefits. In order to receive such benefits, the victim-survivor must apply or prepare to apply for federal U nonimmigrant status, which requires being helpful in an investigation against an offender (8 U.S.C. 1101[a][15][U]). This part is a carceral goal. When we unwrap the classed benefit tradeoff for pursuing the political, carceral end, we expose that the social honor of IMR victim-survivors of IPV becomes relegated to a "tool" to be used by the State. This relegation of certain human beings to the status of a "tool" to meet the state's political and economic objectives of social control represents a partial objectification of a group that already deals with violence and surveillance in the relationship context.

Second, some themes from the current study and the extant literature work together to tell a story of poly-survivorship. It has been described that many victim-survivors of violence will experience multiple "types" of violence (e.g., physical, psychological, sexual) in their lives through poly victimization (Finkelhor, Ormrod, & Turner, 2007; for additional discussions, see also Hamby & Grych, 2013; Montanez, Donley, & Reckdenwald, 2020). At the interpersonal level, all 72 statutes are related to domestic or family violence, which is an interpersonal phenomenon when viewed through a micro lens. Additionally, in Chapter Seven's discussion of empathy and public policy, 52 percent of issue-mentioning statutes discussed "Other Topics" acknowledging hardship including interpersonal ones, such as psychological trauma (Cal Gov Code 13963.1) and needing immigration documents returned by parties being served with protection orders (NY CLS Fam Ct Act § 842). With only 11 percent of total statutes shifting resources from government entities to social services or survivors, the journey through these issues may be compounded by victim-survivors' having to navigate them without (for the most part) direct resource provision at the statute level (see Chapter 8). At the same time, IPV victim-survivors are subject to poly-victimization that extends outside of the interpersonal level to include the institutional and structural levels as well (see Guadalupe-Diaz & West, 2020).

To illuminate further, Guadalupe-Diaz and West (2020) recollect the story of Ms. Gonzáles, whose experience of trying to seek legal protection in the context of IPV resulted in detention by immigration authorities and highlights the vulnerabilities of transgender immigrant IPV victim-survivors across interpersonal, institutional, and structural levels. These dynamics are acknowledged even if symbolically by the state of Washington, in which it is stated that crime victims, including victims of domestic violence, have reluctance in approaching formal authorities for help regarding their situations (Wash. Rev. Code § 7.98.005). Victim-survivors may be fearful of dealing with potential institutional violence (e.g., detention) while attempting to claim freedom from interpersonal violence (IPV). Potential intersections with structural violence such as poverty in the lives of victim-survivors of IPV and violence more generally (see Harrell, Langton, Berzofsky, Couzens, & Smiley-McDonald, 2014; Jasinski, Wesely, Wright, & Mustaine, 2010; Raphael, 2000) hold the potential to compound possible institutional and interpersonal violence. Thus, when we unwrap political and economic contexts, IMR victim-survivors of IPV can be characterized as having the status of poly-survivors, whereby interpersonal victimization itself confers a status (e.g., between victim and offender), which triggers and overlaps with victimization from other levels.

Third, victimization terms are often spoken by statutes in the presence of adjectives that define the parameters of eligibility, worthiness, humanity, and existence. For example, in defining the parameters of eligibility and worthiness, some statutes use terms like "eligible alien" (N.J. Stat. § 30:4D-3) and "qualified aliens" (Conn. Gen. Stat. § 17b-112c). Some statutes defined the parameters of humanity; In another example, while "undocumented immigrant" (Minn Stat. § 256J.11) is used within a statute, others use terms like "illegal aliens" (N.J. Stat. § 44:10-48) and "unauthorized alien" (Ala. Code § 31-13-3).

Some statutes define the parameters of existence or what it means to have a place in society, such as the terms "questionable status" (Conn. Gen. Stat. § 17b-342), "illegal presence," and "unlawful entry" (S.C. Code. Ann. § 16-9-460). These are inherently political terms, which allocate economic and economics-intersecting resources like public benefits or protection from violence-perpetrating partners that could prove invaluable in attaining freedom from abuse and the State. When we peel back these political and economic contexts, we find that IMR victim-survivors of IPV, depending on their particular configurations of identity and label (e.g., permanent resident victim-survivor of psychological IPV, undocumented victim-survivor of physical dating violence) have varied stigmatized statuses that become apparent when placing them under particularly negative attitudinal climates toward immigration in general. The terms victim and survivor already come with connotations based on perceived levels of agency (see Leisenring, 2006). Moreover, victim-survivors must often prove themselves "worthy" of protection/support through constructing narratives that cherry-pick their life experiences (Sweet, 2019) and/or reconjure the memory of painful experiences (Abassi, 2020). Furthermore, certain immigration statuses, legally and informally through public attitudes, confer different levels of stigma. Intersections among these dynamics create various constellations of social honor, which are further disaggregated by raced, classed, and gendered variations in resource allocation that underpin the U.S. simultaneously categorical, multiplicative, and intersecting stratifying and oppressive systems.

Other labels and characteristics put forth by some statutes painted a picture of the social status of IMR victim-survivors of IPV. For example, some statutes describe the situation of certain domestic violence victims as "underserved" (Cal. Pen. Code § 13823.17) or compare them to "non-marginalized" communities, implying their marginalization (ALM GL ch. 12, § 33). These descriptions give hints as to the treatment of such victim-survivors.

Discussion

This chapter looked at how statutes shape the statutes (or social honor) of IMR victim-survivors of IPV. First, the law uses victim-survivors as tools to meet the State's carceral goals. Second, in navigating interpersonal, institutional, and structural violence, victim-survivors become poly-survivors: not only surviving physical, sexual, and/or psychological abuse but also jumping through systemic "hoops" and trudging through broader harmful conditions. Third, in being pinned between victimization status and immigration status, victim-survivors become variously stigmatized, especially when one considers the broader, extant pervasiveness of both xenophobic and victim-blaming attitudes.

However, the statutes do not tell us about the extra-legal ways in which social honor is bestowed and experienced. They do not tell us about the blame and shame (see, e.g., Sabri et al., 2018), the fear experienced, the pressure to keep an intact family unit (see, e.g., Watcher, Cook Heffron, Dalpe, & Spitz, 2020), or rejection by an encompassing community (see, e.g., Silva-Martínez, 2016; for more information on these and other phenomena, see Chapter 10). These are all indicators of positionality and treatment in the stratification system.

Conclusion

Through categorization, humans segment other humans into groups and paint such groups with varying social values that are accompanied by unequal resource allocation (see Massey, 2007). In this context, power is stratified based on class and status—that is, social honor (see Weber, 1925/2008). In the U.S., stratification is multi-pronged and interlocking (see Collins & Bilge, 2020; Massey, 2007). Under this system of stratification, IMR victim-survivors of IPV may hold various positionalities that color and bestow their social honor. As shown by the current analysis, the law uses such victim-survivors as tools to meet State goals. Victim-survivors are also poly-survivors, navigating multiple levels of dangerous victimization terrain. Finally, IMR victim-survivors of IPV navigate various labels and identities that contour their experiences and needs as worthy/unworthy and having agency/not having agency, all alongside the possibility of stigmatized immigration labels. While the statutes cannot tell us about the extralegal dimensions of social honor applied to the lived experiences of IMR victim-survivors of IPV, they set the foundation for understanding the nexus of the formal and informal worlds.

References

Abassi, G. (2020). Discipline and commoditize: How u-visas exploit the pain of gender-based violence. *Feminist Criminology*, *15*(4), 464–491.

Collins, P. H., & Bilge, S. (2020). *Intersectionality.* Medford, MA: Polity Press.

Elliot, J. (n.d.). *Jane Elliot.* Retrieved from https://janeelliott.com/

Finkelhor, D., Ormrod, R. K., & Turner, H. A. (2007, January). Poly-victimization: A neglected component in child victimization. *Child Abuse & Neglect*, *31*(1), 7–26.

Guadalupe-Diaz, X. L., & West, C. M. (2020). The intersections of race and immigration. In A. M. Messinger, & X. L. Guadalupe-Diaz (Eds.), *Transgender intimate partner violence: A comprehensive introduction.* New York, NY: New York University Press.

Hamby, S., & Grych, J. (2013). *The web of violence: Exploring connections among different forms of interpersonal violence and abuse.* New York and London: Springer.

Harrell, E., Langton, L., Berzofsky, M., Couzens, L., & Smiley-McDonald, H. (2014). Household poverty and nonfatal violent victimization, 2008-2012. Bureau of Justice Statistics. Retrieved from https://www.bjs.gov/content/pub/pdf/hpnvv0812.pdf

Jasinski, J. L., Wesely, J. K., Wright, J. D., & Mustaine, E. E. (2010). *Hard lives, mean streets: Violence in the lives of homeless women.* Lebanon, NH: Northeastern University Press.

Leisenring, A. (2006). Confronting "victim" discourses: The identity work of battered women. *Symbolic Interaction, 29*(3), 307–330.

Massey, D. S. (2007). *Categorically unequal: The American stratification system.* New York, NY: Russel Sage Foundation.

Montanez, J., Donley, A., & Reckdenwald, A. (2020). Intersecting dimensions of violence, abuse and victimization. In H. Pontell (Ed.), *Oxford research encyclopedia of criminology and criminal justice.* New York and Oxford: Oxford University Press. doi: 10.1093/acrefore/9780190264079.013.687

PBS. (2003, January 1). A class divided: Introduction. *Frontline.* Retrieved from https://www.pbs.org/wgbh/frontline/article/introduction-2/

Raphael, J. (2000). *Saving Bernice: Battered women, welfare, and poverty.* Boston, MA: Northeastern University Press.

Sabri, B., Nnawulezi, N., Njie-Carr, V. P. S., Messing, J., Ward-Lasher, A., Alvarez, C., & Campbell, J. C. (2018). Multilevel risk and protective factors for intimate partner violence among African, Asian, and Latina immigrant and refugee women: Perceptions of effective safety planning interventions. *Race and Social Problems, 10*(4), 348–365.

Silva-Martínez, E. (2016). "El silencio": Conceptualizations of Latina immigrant survivors of intimate partner violence in the Midwest of the United States. *Violence Against Women, 22*(5), 523–544.

Sweet, P. L. (2019). The paradox of legibility: Domestic violence and institutional survivorhood. *Social Problems, 66*, 411–427.

Watcher, K., Cook Heffron, L., Dalpe, J., & Spitz, A. (2020). Where is the women's center here?" The role of information in refugee women's help seeking for intimate partner violence in a resettlement context. *Violence Against Women.* doi: 10.1177/1077801220971364.

Weber, M. (1925/2008). The distribution of power within the political community: Class, status, party. In Appelrouth, S., & Edles, L. D. (Eds.), *Classical and contemporary sociological theory: Text and readings.* Thousand Oaks, CA: Pine Forge Press (pp. 167–175).

10 Conclusion

This book analyzed state-level statutes that target IPV in IMR lives in the U.S. This chapter, the concluding chapter, discusses the main findings of the research. The chapter then makes connections among findings within the previous sections/chapters to discuss what these findings mean for the sociological study of domestic violence law. Contextual phenomena like immigration policies more broadly, as well as a pandemic, are also discussed. We also identify the methodological and theoretical/conceptual limitations of the analysis. Implications for research, prevention, and intervention are discussed accordingly. Finally, conclusions are made to close the chapter.

Main Findings

To summarize, the present research found 72 statutes scattered across 17 U.S. states. These statutes mostly dealt with public benefits or criminal justice/law enforcement. Over one-third mentioned human trafficking. Statutes also mentioned various immigration-related identities (e.g., refugee, permanent resident), which were decorated with various descriptors. The term *victim* was mentioned in several statutes. Statutes also mentioned various federal policy mechanisms, such as the U-visa and the T-visa.

Guided by the concepts of social control and surveillance, the present research found that one-third of statutes imposed requirements in exchange for benefits or protections, such as trading helpfulness for protection. Statute language, which was hypothesized to be ultimately derived from collectivized standpoints that change text and ruling relations, shaped resource access, and eligibility in various ways. Drawing inspiration from intersectionality, the present research found that statutes, overall, were not inclusive and for the most part did not acknowledge demographic intersections.

DOI: 10.4324/9781003167044-10

The present research also incorporated the concepts of empathy and empowerment. Over 40 percent of statutes mentioned or addressed issues that affect IMR victim-survivors of IPV, such as trauma and reluctance to approach law enforcement for assistance. A small number (approximately 11 percent) of statutes shifted resources, such as moving monies from perpetrators to restitution funds to organizations. Finally, the research found various ways in which statute constructed status.

Discussion

Our discussion focuses on contextualizing findings in the study of law, domestic and international developments, and a pandemic.

Laws as Sites of Multiple Ideas

Statutes in the present research had many components and took on various ideas aside from the major subjects/topics under which they were categorized. That is, statutes were not singular in their foci. They were patchworks of different ideas that were woven into the legal text over time. Statutes had various effective dates in which iterations of new ideas were integrated with each effective date. They etched in the legal text the overarching attitudes of certain time periods. For example, sometimes laws concerned public benefits. At other times, they addressed health and budgets. These phenomena lay the groundwork upon which such laws also become sites of competition between discrimination and anti-discrimination forces.

Laws as Sites of Competition among Oppressive and Anti-Discrimination Forces

The two most identified categories of statute subjects regarded public benefits and criminal justice/law enforcement.

- about 42 percent of the statute subjects focused on public benefits;
- approximately 38 percent of statute subjects focused on criminal justice/law enforcement.

This phenomenon may be reflective of a back-and-forth battle over "get tough" policies. In these battles, IMR victims-survivors of IPV are caught in the crossfire between mechanisms like racism, classism, and sexism, and social control, as well as the anti-discrimination forces that aim to dismantle such mechanisms.

Mass incarceration is grounded in anti-Black punitiveness that perpetually and oppressively watches and punishes. After Emancipation, a few constitutional amendments abolished slavery. The Reconstruction period that followed was dismantled through strategies like Black Codes and criminal/penal systems. Jim Crow Laws then offered a renewed means of domination. In the 1950s and 1960s, major subnational units in the U.S. pushed back against civil rights mobilization. Policing powers were militarized and decorated with weapons that would have only been appropriate for war. The 1980s featured a grander effort to incapacitate and impose law and order on communities. Over this time, the "war on crime and drugs" shifted toward a "war on gangs." These dynamics built further and resulted in the 1994 passage of the Violent Crime Control and Law Enforcement Act (Hinton & Cook, 2021).

During the war on poverty, social spending increased substantially. However, over the course of the 1970s and 1980s, social spending decreased and eventually flat-lined (Massey, 2007). In 1996, the Personal Responsibility and Work Opportunity Reconciliation Act was enshrined into law, "essentially forcing mothers of dependent children off of welfare rolls and into the labor force by ending the entitlement to open-ended income transfers" (p. 171). These transformations over time represent a trend toward "pulling the rug" from underneath the feet of society's most economically vulnerable.

With regard to immigration, over time, there was a shift from border enforcement to interior enforcement (Golash-Boza, 2016; Massey, 2007); additionally, this shift also featured a shift toward deporting people who were a part of family units (Golash-Boza, 2016). Overall, there were four features of social, political, and economic systems that underpinned "mass deportation": a majority of deportees' being Latin American and Caribbean men; a post-9/11 political climate characterized by fear; a worldwide financial downturn; and the economic utility of deportable persons. These results were supercharged by anti-terrorism and unauthorized immigration laws, most notably the Illegal Immigration Reform and Immigrant Responsibility Act of 1996 (Golash-Boza, 2016).

These three forces—public benefits restriction, immigration control, and mass incarceration—intertwined in the 1990s to form a context of risk for IMR victim-survivors of IPV. Developing parallel to these developments was the development of the battered women's movement with its modern origins in the 1970s (Barner & Carney, 2011; Barnett, Miller-Perrin, & Perrin, 2011), with different forms of violence gaining recognition from that time forward (Barnett et al., 2011).

This parallel directionality turned perpendicular as the anti-domestic violence movement paired with the carceral system (Goodmark, 2018; Richie, 2012).

The statutes tell the story. These statutes are immigration-related laws that target the criminal legal system and public benefits control. It is at this nexus that we see discrimination and anti-discrimination forces spar on the 50-state legal battlefield. Section 8-29-10 of Annotated Code of South Carolina set forth eligibility for public social services. Setting IPV aside, the statute is positioned at the intersection of immigration control and public benefits. The State brings in mechanisms reminiscent of mass incarceration and social control (whether for good or bad), a felony penalty, and verification of lawful status. However, there is a site of resistance within the statute where verification of status is not required for certain aspects of assistance under VAWA and other laws: "benefits, programs, services, or any other assistance provided to victims of domestic violence, irrespective of their immigration status, under the Violence Against Women Act of 2000..." (S.C. Code § 8-29-10). In this statute, we see immigration control, public benefit restriction, and carceral efforts spar with a progressive force (services under VAWA that exempt from status verification). Metaphorically speaking, in state-level statutes targeting IPV against IMR persons, public benefit and criminal justice provisions form the chessboard upon which immigration-violence statutes are the chess pieces, with conservative and progressive forces engaged in a game that is emblematic of a structural fight over resources and protection.

Political Climates, International Developments, and Immigration Politics

The present research started in late 2018 in which restrictionist immigration rhetoric and actions were topical and at the forefront in the U.S. and beyond. In 2017, executive actions such as travel bans and the announcing of border wall construction were just the start. In April 2018, a "Zero Tolerance Policy" was put forth in the U.S. Under this policy, thousands of migrant children were separated from their family units (Buchanan, Woglin, & Flores, 2021). In late October 2018, the 45th president stated an intention to end birthright citizenship (Flores & King, 2019). The U.S. was not the only place on the earth in which xenophobic rhetoric and actions were taking place. Preceding the time period, in addition to the installation of the U.S.'s 45th president, populist forces had arisen and had powerful impacts on the political landscape of many Western countries. For example, in 2016, populist forces became the driving force in the British referendum to leave the European Union. The rise of populist forces was a long-festering phenomenon. Segments of Western countries felt left behind and threatened by increased calls for ideals like gender, racial, and LGBT equality. The perceived degradation of the traditional ways of going about life triggered a "cultural backlash" that gave rise to populist forces, which were propelled forward by anti-immigration sentiments (see Inglehart & Norris, 2016).

As previously stated, immigration politics has shifted many times (see Massey, 2007; Golash-Boza, 2016). Increasingly, to stop and suppress migration flows, receiving countries are regulating areas outside of their geographic boundaries through the externalization of migration controls to deem those seeking help as inadmissible even before they reach their intended destination (Frelick, Kysel, & Podkul, 2018). This holds the potential to be salient in the context of asylum seeking. In 2018, the U.S. Attorney General stated that domestic violence, in addition to gang violence, would be excluded as reason for asylum (Flores, 2018). Showing that domestic violence victimization status qualifies as a "particular social group" in asylum law poses a challenge enough (Bachmair, 2015; Bookey, 2016; McKinnon, 2016). Looking at gender as a political category, the universality of male-assigned sex and the silo-ing of gender from other political categories (e.g., race, religion) in U.S. asylum law erases the context that violence against women is a byproduct of the intersection of *all* other political categories (e.g., race, religion; McKinnon, 2016). Intersecting with externalizing migration controls, one question is whether domestic violence victim-survivors have a difficult time presenting their claims.

The Pandemic

Data collection, coding, and analysis finished in October 2021. The last leg of the research project occurred during the time in which a pandemic—Severe Acute Respiratory Syndrome Coronavirus 2, causative of COVID-19 or "coronavirus"—swept across the globe. The pandemic, at the time we are writing this book, has killed over 600,000 people in the U.S (Bacon, Aspegren, & Ortiz, 2021). In addition to laying bare health and income inequalities, the U.S.'s policy response and fragmented pre-existing social service and health care infrastructure have opened the floodgates for a barrage of harmful effects that accompany IPV, which has come to be known as "a pandemic within a pandemic" (Evans, Lindauer, & Farrell, 2020).

There are various occurrences and phenomena that could potentially wrap around the experiences of IMR victim-survivors of IPV. For example,

- A study by Piquero, Jennings, Jemison, Kaukinen, and Knaul (2021), which studied the relationship between lockdowns and domestic violence across various studies, found that stay-at-home/lockdown orders were strongly associated with an increase in domestic violence incidents.
- Foreign-born persons are estimated to constitute six million of the workers in "frontline" industries (e.g., health care) that are important for keeping society functioning during the pandemic (Gelat, 2020). During the pandemic, these situations were also sites of increased risk for catching the virus.
- Compounding stressors infiltrated the lives of IPV victim-survivors during the pandemic. For example, according to Lyons and Brewer's (2021) study, a perpetrator was reported to use a fake diagnosis to stop a victim's air travel. It was reported that domestic violence shelters reached full capacity. The pandemic delayed planned escape from abuse. One discussion showed a victim being "stuck" with a violence-perpetrating partner.

Sabri et al. (2020), which looked at the experiences of immigrant IPV victim-survivors during the pandemic, found a number of themes that echoed the aforementioned phenomena. For example, some women noted increased financial stress and the inability to leave violent situations. Indeed, the pandemic may have made conditions worse for IMR victim-survivors of IPV.

Limitations

The research within this book did include some limitations. First, interviews with IMR victim-survivors of IPV were not conducted by the researchers, meaning that the research relied on previously published studies to draw conclusions. Second, there is a chance that, with the present research's statute search strategy, existing IMR-IPV statutes may have evaded its methodological catchment. Third, the findings of the book were the product of the specific frameworks utilized. With a different set of frameworks, a different set of findings may have been found, with a different set of conclusions drawn. Finally, the present research has limits to its reach in terms of scope. That is, since the focus was on state-level statutes, its implications may not translate smoothly into federal policy, as well as executive and judicial policy.

Implications

Research

Regardless, the present research fills a gap in the literature. In addition to adding to the literature on IPV against IMR individuals, it also adds an examination to the study of laws aiming to help IMR victim-survivors of IPV. Indeed, there have been many works looking at the federal level laws. This examination, to our knowledge, is one of the firsts to excavate and subsequently analyze various *state-level* laws targeting IPV against IMR individuals (see also Kamhi & Lakhani, 2020). Additionally, future research could gauge the usage of the statutes within the current research. Specifically, research questions could be formulated around whether victims are using statute-created programs or whether these statutes are showing up in court cases. Such possibilities for future research can lay the groundwork for assessing the impact of these laws. The list of IMR-related IPV statutes can also be used to measure the impact of public policy on social issues. One work describing the impact of SB 1070 on a predominantly Latino neighborhood discussed a chilling effect in relation to violence:

> Legal professionals we interviewed also anticipated a drop in the propensity of residents to report domestic violence or apply for U visas, which provide temporary legal status to victims of violence under the Victims of Trafficking and Violence Protection Act of 2000[20] (HR 3244). SB 1070, then, likely inadvertently affected rates of substance abuse and domestic violence in the neighborhood
>
> (Hardy et al., 2012, p. 1252).

Considering these and other issues, the authors state the need to broaden the scientific investigation of the public health burden of immigration policies. IMR-related IPV laws should be an integral part of such policy analysis.

Prevention

Inequalities form the contextual foundation upon which violence is more easily allowed to start and flourish. Where possible, to foster the prevention of IPV, non-IPV-IMR laws must change to mitigate inequalities that catalyze violence. For example, Campbell, Rothman, Shareef, and Siegel (2019) found that, across states within the U.S., intimate partner homicide increased as gender inequity increased. Indeed, proactive steps to mitigate gender, racial, and class inequalities would help to mitigate the risk of IPV before it occurs.

Intervention

While statutes took on several topics (e.g., law enforcement/criminal justice, health, public benefits) and acknowledged many issues (e.g., reluctance to contact law enforcement, trauma), some things are difficult or impossible to legally remediate; whether they should or should not be treated with legal tools is up for debate. For example, with certain definitions of domestic violence, family violence, and other terms, laws excluding emotional abuse block the ability to direct services to survivors before abuse escalates. Those victim-centered interventions, the ones that provide direct aid, are sectioned off from the reach of victim-survivors in general.

In the wake of IPV, many negative events may occur and be situated beyond the law's reach. As Goodmark (2012) puts it, there needs to be a possibility of "finding justice beyond the justice system" (p. 78). Victim-survivors may develop mental health issues. The law cannot heal PTSD. There is a stigma that accompanies being an IPV survivor. The law cannot keep laypersons from holding victim-blaming attitudes. Natural disasters are known empirically to be associated with increased domestic violence. The law cannot stop natural disasters. In a more specific example, one statute within the present research provided grant funding to trauma recovery centers. While the potential helpfulness of this statute can be seen, the statute itself cannot remediate the emotional and psychological (and physical) residue of trauma. This issue is enhanced for some IMR victim-survivors of IPV. For example, Sabri et al. (2018) discusses the culturally specific layer of violence that contours the experiences of IMR women who experience IPV, such as marriage and divorce expectations, the upholding of a family's image, and community shaming (see also Appendix Table A.4).

As can be seen, there exists a whole world that lies outside of the purview of the law. As such, interventions aiming to ameliorate the wide-ranging effects of IPV must also be able to be deployed without the help of statutes, court cases, or executive action. Bystander intervention must be a priority. Awareness campaigns that show the heart-wrenching realities of what is happening to people's mothers, daughters, aunts, and sisters must also be brought to the forefront. Engaging men in the struggle to stop IPV may need to be done in peer groups and lay settings where racist-sexist language permeates everyday discussion and form the foundation for IPV against IMR persons to materialize. With over 80 million people experiencing IPV in the U.S. across the lifespan, it is safe to say that many people know victim-survivors of IPV. Thus, while approaches aiming to enhance the community response is well-argued and need to be deployed, mobilizing communities may not be enough and may need to be supplanted by mobilizing whole populations in terms of size to eradicate IPV and dismantle its contributing social, political, and economic inequalities.

Policy Recommendations

Unhelpful responses by institutions to help survivors can pile on additional difficulties that accompany IPV's human rights violations (see Glass, Rollins, & Bloom, 2009). Moreover, an approach that views battered women as survivors postulates that, since reaching for just one help source should automatically unlock/trigger the swift action of the entire anti-IPV intervention arsenal, it is the intervention system, rather than the victim, that needs "treatment" (Gondolf & Fisher, 1988). In accordance with the present research's findings, as well as findings and arguments made by the extant literature, the following policy recommendations may provide a formidable starting point for constructing a system of dignity for IMR victim-survivors of IPV.

Acknowledge Struggles, Follow Up with Action

Our analysis of empathy in state-level statutes revealed that some laws engage in certain actions with the acknowledgment of issues that may impact victim-survivors (see Chapter 7). For example, Section 7.98.005 of the Revised Code of Washington acknowledges the reluctance of IMR victim-survivors of IPV to even contact law enforcement when victimized. Indeed, while some state governments are more helpful than others, they are still a part of—and complicit in—the overarching immigration system that spans both federal and state levels. The construction of future state statutes should include preambles or reasoning for actionable provisions—specifically to acknowledge the harm done (see, e.g., Rev. Code. Wash. 7.98.005). While these acknowledgments would be mostly symbolic, it holds the State accountable for the systemic failures that leave victim-survivors vulnerable. At the same time, if an issue is acknowledged, there must be an appropriate prescription to remediate the hardship.

Believe Survivors by Eliminating Transactional Means of Cultivating Protection

Our analysis of surveillance and social control revealed that some laws require IMR victim-survivors to "trade" some character signifier or attribute for resources and protection (see Chapter 4). From our findings, we recommend that resource and protection provision should not be conditioned on actions/attributes such as "helpfulness." Policies should be revised or recreated to respond to victim status, *not* victim status *plus* character attributes. Victim-survivors often have to navigate attitudinal and legal terrains that do not readily believe or give serious thought to their victimization experiences. They may face victim-blaming, not being believed, or told that abuse is a "private" matter. It would better serve victim-survivors to believe them—specifically, by removing the additional character hoops through which they have to jump to construct narratives that frame them as "worthy" of support.

Institute Hardship-Informed Survivor-Centeredness

IMR victim-survivors of IPV experience contextual occurrences that impact and complicate violent experiences (e.g., reluctance to contact law enforcement, the risk of being abandoned by one's community, the pressure to preserve the family image). The very mention of these concerns, as well as violence itself, should automatically unlock resources, services, and protection. Messing et al. (2016) discuss the Lethality Assessment Program, which first identifies the potential for the risk of homicide, then based on that assessment, potentially leads to a connection to services and safety planning. A similar pathway should be provided for IMR victim-survivors of IPV and etched into legal texts. For example, a statute could state a lengthy series of issues faced by IMR victim-survivors of various backgrounds. Such issues could serve as keys to obtaining resources. This would help in various situations.

- First, violence may not be occurring every second of the day. However, although violence may not be happening in the immediate time period, concerns surrounding the IPV-IMR nexus could still be present (e.g., being scared to reach out to authorities). The aforementioned remedy would help in this situation by allowing victims-survivors to obtain resources and protection without having to prove physical or sexual battering.

- Second, IMR victim-survivors of different backgrounds can have different concerns based on contexts like culture (see, e.g., Sabri et al., 2018). In this case, having a list of hardships within a statute that unlock resource/protection provision could help the law come closer to sensing experiences through an intersectional lens.

However, such a step would require enhanced effort. That is, it would need to draw from the extant research on the IMR-IPV nexus. This would mean that research would need to be more easily translated into public policy, especially if there is attitudinal and electoral support for IMR in general.

Conclusion

This book examined state-level statutes that target IPV against IMR individuals. Indeed, in the absence of IPV, IMR persons can experience a complicated maze of navigating the U.S.'s legal terrain. In the absence of IMR status, IPV victim-survivors such as the U.S.-born citizen victim-survivors already experience unspeakable abuse, including strangulation, kidnapping, and being killed. The intersection of these two statuses, the IMR-IPV nexus, includes compounded and unique occurrences, such as feeling cornered between systems and violence. These experiences are further nuanced and compounded by other positions IMR victim-survivors may hold in society, for example, at the axis of race, class, gender (identity), sexuality, ability, and other statuses.

Accordingly, the legal labyrinth through which IMR victim-survivors of IPV may journey is also a site of complexity, as well as setting into which oppressive forces can inject inequality. However, this terrain is simultaneously a space in which anti-discrimination forces can harness the power of law as a resistance mechanism to dilute and overpower inequality's hold on the criminal and civil legal systems. In this way, the law can be used to affect the change that helps mitigate interpersonal violence while checking State power.

References

Bachmair, J. K. (2015). Asylum at last?: Matter of A-R-C-G-'s impact on domestic violence victims seeking asylum. *Cornell Law Review*, *101*, 1053–1085.

Bacon, J., Aspegren, E., & Ortiz, J. L. (2021, June 15). US surpasses 600,000 deaths from the coronavirus; California reopens: Latest COVID-19 updates. *USA Today*. Retrieved from https://www.usatoday.com/story/news/health/2021/06/15/covid-vaccine-variant-restrictions-california-deaths/7695348002/

Barner, J. R., & Carney, M. M. (2011). Interventions for intimate partner violence: A historical review. *Journal of Family Violence, 26*(3), 235–244.

Barnett, O. W., Miller-Perrin, C. L., & Perrin, R. D. (2011). *Family violence across the lifespan: An introduction* (3rd ed.). Thousand Oaks, CA: SAGE Publications, Inc.

Bookey, B. (2016). Gender-based asylum post-matter of a-r-c-g: Evolving standards and fair application of the law. *Southwestern Journal of International Law, 22*, 1–19.

Buchanan, M. J., Wolgin, P. E., & Flores, C. (2021, April 12). The Trump administration's family separation policy is over: What comes next? *Center for American Progress*. Retrieved from https://www.americanprogress.org/issues/immigration/reports/2021/04/12/497999/trump-administrations-family-separation-policy/

Campbell, J. K., Rothman, E. F., Shareef, F., & Siegel, M. B. (2019). The relative risk of intimate partner and other homicide victimization by state-level gender inequity in the United States, 2000-2017. *Violence & Gender, 6*(4), 211–218.

Evans, M. L., Lindauer, M., & Farrell, M. E. (2020, December 10). A pandemic within a pandemic–Intimate partner violence during COVID-19. *New England Journal of Medicine, 383*, 2302–2304. doi: 10.1056/NEJMp2024046

Flores, A. (2018, June 11). In a major change in US policy, Sessions rules that domestic violence is not grounds for asylum. *Buzz Feed News*. Retrieved from https://www.buzzfeednews.com/article/adolfoflores/sessions-domestic-violence-asylum-immigration

Flores, A., & King, B. (2019, January 8). A timeline of Trump's immigration policies and events. *BuzzFeed News*. Retrieved from https://www.buzzfeednews.com/article/adolfoflores/trump-immigration-policies-defeats-wins

Frelick, B., Kysel, I. M., & Podkul, J. (2018). The impact of externalization of migration controls on the rights of asylum seekers and other migrants. *Journal on Migration and Human Security, 4*(4), 190–220.

Gelat, D. (2020, April). *Immigrant workers: Vital to the U.S. COVID-19 response, disproportionately vulnerable*. Washington, D.C: Migration Policy Institute.

Glass, N., Rollins, C., & Bloom, T. (2009). Expanding our vision: Using a human rights framework to strengthen our service response to female victims of male intimate partner violence. In D. J. Whitaker & J. R. Lutzker (Eds.), *Preventing partner violence: Research and evidence-based intervention strategies* (pp. 193–217). doi: 10.1037/11873-009

Golash-Boza, T. (2016). The parallels between mass incarceration and mass deportation: An intersectional analysis of state repression. *Journal of World-Systems Research, 22*(2), 484–509.

Gondolf, E. W., & Fisher, E. R. (1988). *Battered women as survivors: An alternative to treating learned helplessness.* Massachusetts, MA: Lexington Books.

Goodmark, L. (2012). *A troubled marriage: Domestic violence and the legal system.* New York and London: New York University Press.

Goodmark, L. (2018). *Decriminalizing domestic violence: A balanced policy approach to intimate partner violence.* Oakland, CA: University of California Press.

Hardy, L. J., Getrich, C. M., Quezada, J. C., Guay, A., Michalowski, R. J., & Henley, E. (2012). A call for further research on the impact of state-level immigration policies on public health. *American Journal of Public Health, 102*(7), 1250–1253.

Hinton, E., & Cook, D. (2021). The mass criminalization of Black Americans: A historical overview. *Annual Review of Criminology, 4*, 261–286.

Inglehart, R., & Norris, P. (2016, August). *Trump, Brexit, and the rise of populism: Economic have-nots and cultural backlash.* HKS Faculty Research Working Paper Series RWP16-026. Retrieved from https://www.hks.harvard.edu/publications/trump-brexit-and-rise-populism-economic-have-nots-and-cultural-backlash

Kamhi, A., & Lakhani, S. (2020, April). A guide to state laws on U visa and T visa certifications. *Immigrant legal resource center.* Retrieved from https://www.ilrc.org/sites/default/files/resources/u_visa_and_t_visa_pa-04.2020.pdf

Lyons, M., & Brewer, G. (2021). Experiences of intimate partner violence during lockdown and the COVID-19 pandemic. *Journal of Family Violence.* [Advance online publication]. doi: 10.1007/s10896-021-00260-x.

McKinnon, S. L. (2016). *Gendered asylum: Race and violence in U.S. law and politics.* Urbana, Chicago, and Springfield, IL: University of Illinois Press.

Messing, J. T., Campbell, J. C., Ward-Lasher, A., Brown, S., Patchell, B., & Wilson, J. S. (2016). The lethality assessment program: Which survivors of intimate partner violence are most likely to participate? *Policing: An International Journal of Police Strategies and Management, 39*(1), 64–77.

Piquero, A. R., Jennings, W. G., Jemison, E., Kaukinen, C., & Knaul, F. M. (2021). Domestic violence during the COVID-19 pandemic - evidence from a systematic review and meta-analysis. *Journal of Criminal Justice.*

Sabri, B., Hartley, M., Saha, J., Murray, S., Glass, N., & Campbell, J. C. (2020). Effective of COVID-19 pandemic on women's health and safety: A study of immigrant survivors of intimate partner violence. *Health Care for Women International, 41*, 1294–1312. doi: 10.1080/07399332.2020.1833012

Sabri, B., Nnawulezi, N., Njie-Carr, V. P., Messing, J., Ward-Lasher, A., Alvarez, C., & Campbell, J. C. (2018). Multilevel risk and protective factors for intimate partner violence among African, Asian, and Latina immigrant and refugee women: Perceptions of effective safety planning interventions. *Race and Social Problems, 10*(4), 348–365.

Appendix

Tables for Chapter 2

Table A.1 Search Terminology Combinations Utilized in Statute Search

Immigrant + Abuse
Immigrant + Domestic Violence
Immigrant + Family Violence
Immigrant + Partner Violence
Immigrant + Domestic Abuse
Immigrant + Domestic Dispute
Immigrant + Battered
Immigrant + Violence Against Women
Immigrant + Relationship Violence
Alien + Abuse
Alien + Domestic Violence
Alien + Family Violence
Alien + Partner Violence
Alien + Domestic Abuse
Alien + Domestic Dispute
Alien + Battered
Alien + Violence Against Women
Alien + Relationship Violence
Permanent Resident + Immigrant
Permanent Resident + Abuse
Permanent Resident + Domestic
 Violence
Permanent Resident + Family Violence
Permanent Resident + Partner Violence
Permanent Resident + Domestic Abuse
Permanent Resident + Domestic
 Dispute
Permanent Resident + Battered
Permanent Resident + Violence
 Against Women

Noncitizen + Relationship Violence
Citizen + Abuse
Citizen + Domestic Violence
Citizen + Family Violence
Citizen + Partner Violence
Citizen + Domestic Abuse
Citizen + Domestic Dispute
Citizen + Battered
Citizen + Violence Against Women
Citizen + Relationship Violence
Nonimmigrant + Abuse
Nonimmigrant + Domestic Violence
Nonimmigrant + Family Violence
Nonimmigrant + Partner Violence
Nonimmigrant + Domestic Abuse
Nonimmigrant + Domestic Dispute
Nonimmigrant + Battered
Nonimmigrant + Violence Against
 Women
Nonimmigrant + Relationship Violence
Deeming + Abuse
Deeming + Domestic Violence
Deeming + Family Violence
Deeming + Partner Violence
Deeming + Domestic Abuse
Deeming + Domestic Dispute
Deeming + Battered
Deeming + Violence Against Women
Deeming + Relationship Violence
Undocumented + Abuse

(*Continued*)

122   *Appendix*

Table A.1 Search Terminology Combinations Utilized in Statute Search
(*Continued*)

Permanent Resident + Relationship Violence	Undocumented + Domestic Violence
Refugee + Abuse	Undocumented + Family Violence
Refugee + Domestic Violence	Undocumented + Partner Violence
Refugee + Family Violence	Undocumented + Domestic Abuse
Refugee + Partner Violence	Undocumented + Domestic Dispute
Refugee + Domestic Abuse	Undocumented + Battered
Refugee + Domestic Dispute	Undocumented + Violence Against Women
Refugee + Battered	Undocumented + Relationship Violence
Refugee + Violence Against Women	Asylee + Abuse
Refugee + Relationship Violence	Asylee + Domestic Violence
Noncitizen + Abuse	Asylee + Family Violence
Noncitizen + Domestic Violence	Asylee + Partner Violence
Noncitizen + Family Violence	Asylee + Domestic Abuse
Noncitizen + Partner Violence	Asylee + Domestic Dispute
Noncitizen + Domestic Abuse	Asylee + Battered
Noncitizen + Domestic Dispute	Asylee + Violence Against Women
Noncitizen + Battered	Asylee + Relationship Violence
Noncitizen + Violence Against Women	

Table A.2 List of State-Level Statutes Concerning Immigrant and Refugee
Survivors of Intimate Partner Violence

Statute	*State*
AL Code § 31-13-7	AL
Code of Ala. § 31-13-3	AL
A.C.A. 9-13-408	AR
Cal Fam Code § 1816	CA
Cal Gov Code § 13963.1	CA
Cal Gov Code § 13963.2	CA
Cal Pen Code § 13823.17	CA
Cal Pen Code § 1463.27	CA
Cal Pen Code § 679.10	CA
Cal Wel & Inst Code § 10609.97	CA
Cal Wel & Inst Code § 13283	CA
Cal Wel & Inst Code § 13301	CA
Cal Wel & Inst Code § 13303	CA
Cal Wel & Inst Code § 13305	CA
Cal Wel & Inst Code § 13306	CA
Cal Wel & Inst Code § 13307	CA
Cal Wel & Inst Code § 14005.2	CA
Cal Wel & Inst Code § 18930	CA
Cal Wel & Inst Code § 18932	CA
Cal Wel & Inst Code § 18938	CA
Cal Wel & Inst Code § 18940	CA
Cal Wel & Inst Code § 18945	CA

(*Continued*)

Table A.2 List of State-Level Statutes Concerning Immigrant and Refugee
Survivors of Intimate Partner Violence (*Continued*)

Statute	*State*
Conn. Gen. Stat. § 17b-112c	CT
Conn. Gen. Stat. § 17b-257b	CT
Conn. Gen. Stat. § 17b-342	CT
Conn. Gen. Stat. § 46b-38b	CT
Conn. Gen. Stat. § 46b-38i	CT
Fla. Stat. § 402.87	FL
Fla. Stat. § 414.095	FL
Fla. Stat. § 908.104	FL
Iowa Code § 239B.2B	IA
305 ILCS 5/1-11	IL
305 ILCS 5/16-1	IL
305 ILCS 5/16-2	IL
305 ILCS 5/16-3	IL
305 ILCS 5/16-4	IL
305 ILCS 5/16-5	IL
5 ILCS 825/10	IL
5 ILCS 825/15	IL
5 ILCS 825/5	IL
Ind. Code Ann. 5-2-1-9	IN
ALM GL ch. 112, § 264	MA
ALM GL ch. 12, § 33	MA
ALM GL ch. 18, § 33	MA
ALM GL ch. 6, § 116A	MA
Minn. Stat. § 256B.06	MN
Minn. Stat. § 256J.08	MN
Minn. Stat. § 256J.11	MN
Minn. Stat. § 256P.04	MN
N.J. Stat. § 30:4D-3	NJ
N.J. Stat. § 44:10-44	NJ
N.J. Stat. § 44:10-57	NJ
NJ Stat. § 44:10-45	NJ
NJ Stat. § 44:10-48	NJ
NJ Stat. § 44:10-59	NJ
NRS § 125D.180	NV
NY CLS CPL § 530.12	NY
NY CLS Dom Rel § 252	NY
NY CLS Fam Ct Act § 1056	NY
NY CLS Fam Ct Act § 446	NY
NY CLS Fam Ct Act § 551	NY
NY CLS Fam Ct Act § 842	NY
NY CLS Soc Serv § 17	NY
S.C. Code Ann. § 16-9-460	SC
S.C. Code Ann. § 8-29-10	SC
Tex. Fam. Code § 153.502	TX
Rev. Code Wash. § 7.98.005	WA
Rev. Code Wash. § 7.98.020	WA

(*Continued*)

Table A.2 List of State-Level Statutes Concerning Immigrant and Refugee
Survivors of Intimate Partner Violence (*Continued*)

Statute	State
Rev. Code Wash. § 7.98.030	WA
Rev. Code Wash. § 7.98.010	WA
Rev. Code Wash. § 74.08A.010	WA
Wis. Stat. § 49.165	WI

Tables and Figures for Chapter 3

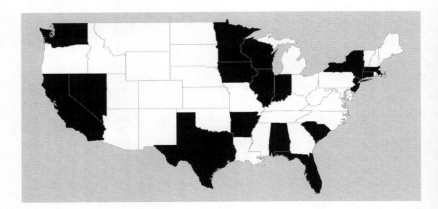

Figure A.1 Map of states that have at least one immigrant and/or refugee-
related intimate partner violence statute. States shaded in black
have at least one immigrant and refugee-related intimate partner
violence statute.

Table A.3 Effective Dates of IPV-Immigration Language
within Statutes (*N* = 72)

Year	n	%[b]
1997	8	11.11
1998	2	2.78
1999	4	5.56
2002	2	2.78
2003	2	2.78
2005	1	1.39
2007	7	9.72
2008	2	2.78
2009	1	1.39
2010	1	1.39

(*Continued*)

Table A.3 Effective Dates of IPV-Immigration Language within Statutes (*N* = 72) (*Continued*)

Year	n	%[b]
2011	2	2.78
2013	8	11.11
2014	3	4.17
2015	2	2.78
2016	8	11.11
2017	2	2.78
2018	5	6.94
2019	4	5.56
Undeterminable[a]	8	11.11

Notes:

a For some statutes, the effective dates of IPV-immigration provisions were unclear. These statutes are as follows: ALM GL ch. 6, § 116A, Conn. Gen. Stat. § 17b-342, Conn. Gen. Stat. § 17b-257b, Conn. Gen. Stat. § 46b-38b, Ind. Code Ann. 5-2-1-9, NJ Stat. § 44:10-48, NJ Stat. § 44:10-59, Wis. Stat. § 49.165.

b This column refers to the percentage of total statutes that have a respective effective date. For example, approximately 11 percent of statutes had IMR IPV provisions that took effect in 1997.

Figures for Chapter 4

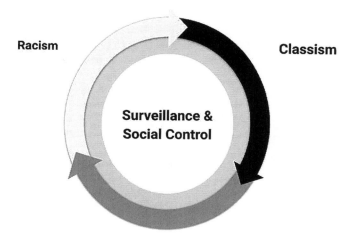

Figure A.2 Depiction of a conceptual model detailing how racism, classism, and sexism interconnect to create surveillance and social control.

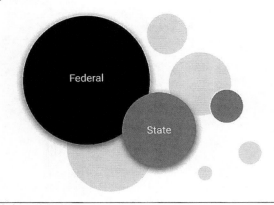

Time

Figure A.3 Depiction of how Statutes decentralize over time cumulatively from federal to subnational.

Figure for Chapter 6

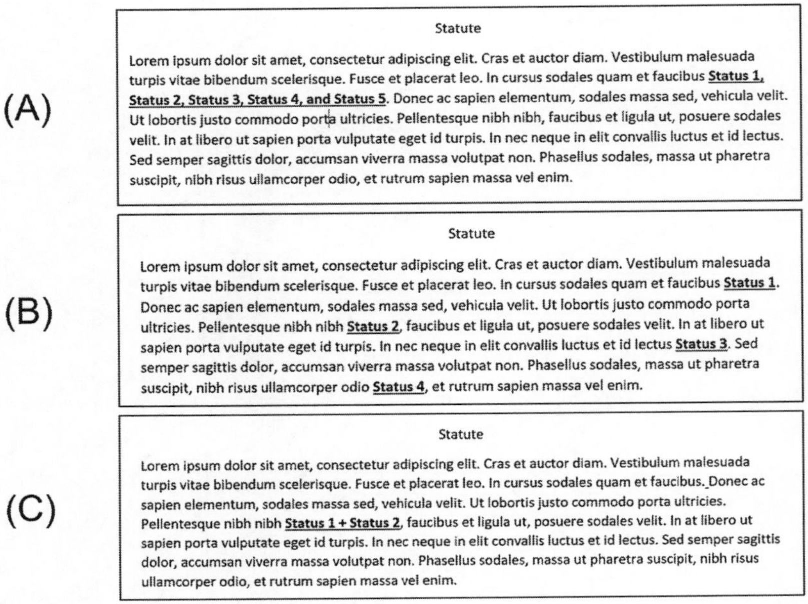

(A)

> **Statute**
>
> Lorem ipsum dolor sit amet, consectetur adipiscing elit. Cras et auctor diam. Vestibulum malesuada turpis vitae bibendum scelerisque. Fusce et placerat leo. In cursus sodales quam et faucibus **Status 1, Status 2, Status 3, Status 4, and Status 5**. Donec ac sapien elementum, sodales massa sed, vehicula velit. Ut lobortis justo commodo porta ultricies. Pellentesque nibh nibh, faucibus et ligula ut, posuere sodales velit. In at libero ut sapien porta vulputate eget id turpis. In nec neque in elit convallis luctus et id lectus. Sed semper sagittis dolor, accumsan viverra massa volutpat non. Phasellus sodales, massa ut pharetra suscipit, nibh risus ullamcorper odio, et rutrum sapien massa vel enim.

(B)

> **Statute**
>
> Lorem ipsum dolor sit amet, consectetur adipiscing elit. Cras et auctor diam. Vestibulum malesuada turpis vitae bibendum scelerisque. Fusce et placerat leo. In cursus sodales quam et faucibus **Status 1**. Donec ac sapien elementum, sodales massa sed, vehicula velit. Ut lobortis justo commodo porta ultricies. Pellentesque nibh nibh **Status 2**, faucibus et ligula ut, posuere sodales velit. In at libero ut sapien porta vulputate eget id turpis. In nec neque in elit convallis luctus et id lectus **Status 3**. Sed semper sagittis dolor, accumsan viverra massa volutpat non. Phasellus sodales, massa ut pharetra suscipit, nibh risus ullamcorper odio **Status 4**, et rutrum sapien massa vel enim.

(C)

> **Statute**
>
> Lorem ipsum dolor sit amet, consectetur adipiscing elit. Cras et auctor diam. Vestibulum malesuada turpis vitae bibendum scelerisque. Fusce et placerat leo. In cursus sodales quam et faucibus. Donec ac sapien elementum, sodales massa sed, vehicula velit. Ut lobortis justo commodo porta ultricies. Pellentesque nibh nibh **Status 1 + Status 2**, faucibus et ligula ut, posuere sodales velit. In at libero ut sapien porta vulputate eget id turpis. In nec neque in elit convallis luctus et id lectus. Sed semper sagittis dolor, accumsan viverra massa volutpat non. Phasellus sodales, massa ut pharetra suscipit, nibh risus ullamcorper odio, et rutrum sapien massa vel enim.

Figure A.4 Depiction of how statutes mention various demographic statuses, identities, backgrounds, and categories.

Appendix Table

Table A.4 Issues Impacting Immigrants and Refugees Affected by Intimate Partner Violence

Issues	*References*
Being Strong	Sabri et al. (2018); Ting (2010)
Blame and Shame	Kallivayalil (2010); Sabri et al. (2018); Shiu-Thornton, Senturia, & Sullivan (2005)
"Blocking Out" Experience	Ting (2010)
Children's Needs	Shiu-Thornton et al. (2005)
Community Attitudes	Akinsulure-Smith, Chu, Keatley, and Rasmussen (2013); Latta and Goodman (2005)
Community Rejection	Silva-Martínez (2016)
Danger in Home Country	Erez, Adelman, and Gregory (2009); Salcido and Adelman (2004); Silva-Martínez (2016); Ting (2010)
Dependence on Partner	Salcido and Adelman (2004)
Economics or Finances	Akinsulure-Smith, Chu, Keatley, and Rasmussen (2013); Wachter, Dalpe, & Heffron (2019)
Gender Topics (e.g., Machismo, Partner Being "King of the Castle")	Alvarez et al. (2021); Kallivayalil (2010); Vidales (2010)
Faith	Ting (2010); Vidales (2010)
Fear	Shiu-Thornton et al. (2005); Wachter et al. (2019)
Fear of Children Being Taken Away	Erez et al. (2009); Kelly (2009); Salcido and Adelman (2004); Silva-Martinez (2016); Vidales (2010)
Friends and Family	Akinsulure-Smith, Chu, Keatley, and Rasmussen (2013); Kyriakakis (2014); Latta and Goodman (2005); Mahapatra and Rai (2019); Reina, Lohman, and Maldonado (2014); Sabri et al. (2018); Salcido and Adelman (2004); Shiu-Thornton et al. (2005); Ting (2010); Vidales (2010)
Isolation	Sabri et al. (2018); Reina et al. (2014)
Keeping the Family Intact	Wachter et al. (2019)
Language	Latta and Goodman (2005); Reina, Lohman, and Maldonado (2014); Shiu-Thornton et al. (2005); Silva-Martínez (2016); Vidales (2010)
Legal Status Issues (e.g., Obtaining Status, Mixed Status Households, Unaware of Rights)	Akinsulure-Smith, Chu, Keatley, and Rasmussen (2013); Alvarez et al. (2021); Bhuyan (2008); Erez et al. (2009); Kallivayalil (2010); Latta and Goodman (2005); Mahapatra and Rai (2019); Reina et al. (2014); Sabri et al. (2018); Salcido and Adelman (2004); Vidales (2010)

(Continued)

Table A.4 Issues Impacting Immigrants and Refugees Affected by Intimate
Partner Violence (*Continued*)

Issues	References
Mental Health (e.g., Suicidal Ideation, Depression)	Erez et al. (2009); Kallivayalil (2010); Shiu-Thornton et al. (2005); Silva-Martínez (2016); Wachter et al. (2019)
Motherhood (e.g., Staying or Leaving for Children's Well-being, Parenting)	Kallivayalil (2010); Kelly (2009); Kyriakakis (2014); Ting (2010)
Optimism	Mahapatra and Rai (2019)
Physical Health	Kallivayalil (2010); Wachter et al. (2019)
Police	Akinsulure-Smith, Chu, Keatley, and Rasmussen (2013); Latta and Goodman (2005)
Poverty and Socioeconomic Status Issues	Vidales (2010)
Pregnancy	Kallivayalil (2010); Sabri et al. (2018)
Presentation of Self (e.g., For Family)	Sabri et al. (2018); Shiu-Thornton et al. (2005); Silva-Martínez (2016)
Racism	Sabri et al. (2018); Silva-Martínez (2016)
Shelter and Service Experiences	Akinsulure-Smith, Chu, Keatley, and Rasmussen (2013); Latta and Goodman (2005); Mahapatra and Rai (2019); Sabri et al. (2018); Ting (2010); Wachter et al. (2019)
Social Contracts	Kallivayalil (2010)
Submission in Order to Protect Self	Silva-Martínez (2016)
Technology	Mahapatra and Rai (2019)
Violence	Akinsulure-Smith, Chu, Keatley, and Rasmussen (2013); Alvarez et al. (2021); Erez et al. (2009); Kallivayalil (2010); Kelly (2009); Mahapatra and Rai (2019); Sabri et al. (2018); Salcido and Adelman (2004); Shiu-Thornton et al. (2005); Silva-Martínez (2016); Ting (2010)
Worry About Deportation/ Removal	Erez et al. (2009); Latta and Goodman (2005); Mahapatra and Rai (2019); Reina et al. (2014); Salcido and Adelman (2004); Silva-Martínez (2016); Vidales (2010)

Notes: Topics in the left column were noted as being present in works authored by authors in the right column. A topic in the left column was noted as being present in a work if the work addressed such a topic in detail or in passing in relation to the text.

References

Akinsulure-Smith, A. M., Chu, T., Keatley, E., & Rasmussen, A. (2013). Intimate partner violence among West African immigrants. *Journal of Aggression, Maltreatment & Trauma*, *22*(2), 109–126.

Alvarez, C., Lameiras-Fernandez, M., Holliday, C. N., Sabri, B., & Campbell, J. (2021). Latina and Caribbean immigrant women's experiences with intimate partner violence: A story of ambivalent sexism. *Journal of Interpersonal Violence*, *36*(7–8), 3831–3854.

Bhuyan, R. (2008). The production of the "battered immigrant" in public policy and domestic violence advocacy. *Journal of Interpersonal Violence*, *23*(2), 153–170.

Erez, E., Adelman, M., & Gregory, C. (2009). Intersections of immigration and domestic violence: Voices of battered immigrant women. *Feminist Criminology*, *4*(1), 32–56.

Kelly, U. A. (2009). "I'm a mother first": The influence of mothering in the decision-making processes of battered immigrant Latino women. *Research in Nursing & Health*, *32*(3), 286–297.

Kyriakakis, S. (2014). Mexican Immigrant women reaching out: The role of informal networks in the process of seeking help for intimate partner violence. *Violence Against Women*, *20*(9), 1097–1116.

Kallivayalil, D. (2010). Narratives of suffering of South Asian immigrant survivors of domestic violence. *Violence Against Women*, *16*(7), 789–811.

Latta, R. E., & Goodman, L. A. (2005). Considering the interplay of cultural context and service provision in intimate partner violence: The case of Haitian immigrant women. *Violence Against Women*, *11*(11), 1441–1464.

Mahapatra, N., & Rai, A. (2019). "Every cloud has a silver lining but…": Pathways to seeking formal-help and South-Asian immigrant women survivors of intimate partner violence". *Health Care for Women International*, *40*(11), 1170–1196.

Reina, A. S., Lohman, B. J., & Maldonado, M. M. (2014). "He said they'd deport me": Factors influencing domestic violence help-seeking practices among Latina immigrants. *Journal of Interpersonal Violence*, *29*(4), 593–615.

Sabri, B., Nnawulezi, N., Njie-Carr, V. P., Messing, J., Ward-Lasher, A., Alvarez, C., & Campbell, J. C. (2018). Multilevel risk and protective factors for intimate partner violence among African, Asian, and Latina immigrant and refugee women: Perceptions of effective safety planning interventions. *Race and Social Problems*, *10*(4), 348–365.

Salcido, O., & Adelman, M. (2004). "He has me tied with the blessed and damned papers": Undocumented-immigrant battered women in Phoenix, Arizona. *Human Organization*, 63(2), 162–172.

Shiu-Thornton, S., Senturia, K., & Sullivan, M. (2005). "Like a bird in a cage": Vietnamese Women survivors talk about domestic violence. *Journal of Interpersonal Violence*, *20*(8), 959–976.

Silva-Martínez, E. (2016). "El silencio": Conceptualizations of Latina immigrant survivors of intimate partner violence in the Midwest of the United States. *Violence Against Women, 22*(5), 523–544.

Ting, L. (2010). Out of Africa: Coping strategies of African immigrant women survivors of intimate partner violence. *Health Care for Women International, 31*(4), 345–364.

Vidales, G. T. (2010). Arrested justice: The multifaceted plight of immigrant Latinas who faced domestic violence. *Journal of Family Violence, 25*(6), 533–544.

Wachter, K., Dalpe, J., & Heffron, L. C. (2019). Conceptualizations of domestic violence–related needs among women who resettled to the United States as refugees. *Social Work Research, 43*(4), 207–219.

Index

Italicized and **bold** pages refer to figures and tables respectively, and page numbers followed by "n" refer to notes.

132   *Index*

For Product Safety Concerns and Information please contact our EU
representative GPSR@taylorandfrancis.com Taylor & Francis Verlag GmbH,
Kaufingerstraße 24, 80331 München, Germany

Printed and bound by CPI Group (UK) Ltd, Croydon, CR0 4YY

11/04/2025

01844003-0007